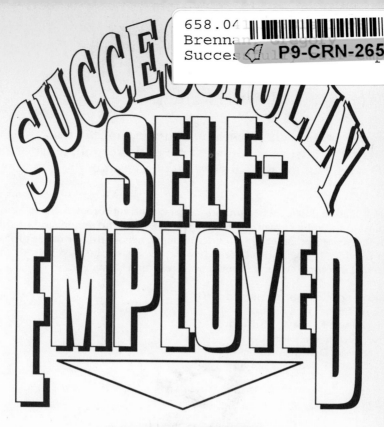

SUCCESSFULLY SELF-EMPLOYED

WITHDRAWN

GREGORY BRENNAN

**UPSTART
PUBLISHING COMPANY**
Specializing in Small Business Publishing
a division of Dearborn Publishing Group, Inc.

7/97

Dedication

To my father, who always encouraged me to read; to my mother, who always encouraged me to write; and, most of all, to my wife, Donna, who always encourages me.

Executive Editor: Bobbye Middendorf
Managing Editor: Jack Kiburz
Project Editor: Karen A. Christensen
Interior Design: Lucy Jenkins
Cover Design: Design Alliance, Inc.
Author Photo: Ed Aiona Photography

© 1996 by Gregory F. Brennan

Published by Upstart Publishing Company,
a division of Dearborn Publishing Group, Inc.

Printed in the United States of America.

96 97 98 10 9 8 7 6 5 4 3 2 1

Library of Congress Cataloging-in-Publication Data

Brennan, Gregory.
    Successfully self-employed : how to sell what you do, do what you
sell, manage your cash in between / Gregory Brennan.
       p.   cm.
    Includes index.
    ISBN 1-57410-000-9 (pbk.)
    1. Self-employed. 2. Small business—Planning. 3. Small
business—Management. I. Title.
HD8036.B73   1996   95-49460
658'.041—dc20   CIP

CONTENTS

PREFACE

You are self-employed, or you are thinking real hard about going out on your own.

You're not alone. As corporate America has become leaner and companies have merged to benefit from "economies of scale," millions of professionals in shoes just your style have found their jobs eliminated. Others left their jobs because they wanted to experience the American dream of being on their own.

Job titles are being erased from organizational charts all across this country, but these jobs still need to be done. Now projects are out-sourced by overwhelmed corporate survivors who *need* you and your skills.

On the surface it seems like you'll do just fine. After all, you've been honing your skills for years. You've won awards for your work. You know what it takes to get the job done.

But there are three hitches. The first—and biggest—hitch: you have to convince someone to bring you on board for a project. Second, you have to do the work. And third, you have to manage the money that you earned until you can land another project. If you don't do these three things well, you better learn—and fast!

That's what I had to do, and that's what this book is about.

In the mid-80s I was working for Bank of America producing and directing corporate video programs. I wanted increased responsibility, but the bank was bleeding to death with losses of more than $1 billion per year. My boss wasn't going to be promoted any time soon, which meant that I wasn't either. I was frustrated by policies and procedures enforced on the staff to try to reduce the bank's losses. Many of the people I highly respected were leaving. It soon became obvious to me that I should, too.

At first, business went well enough that my wife and I built a house. Then things went in the toilet—and it had nothing to do with the plumbing in the new house. The quarter before we moved I netted $27. I realized then that I had to make clients *want* to hire me. It was a rude awakening, but I vowed never to be caught in that position again. Business picked up, and by the end of that year I had earned more than the previous year, which was more than my previous salary had been.

How did I do that? I had a written business plan that was based on more than a decade of my own experience, but I wasn't really certain how to find prospects and turn them into clients. I read a lot of books about how to start a business, about 300 perfect sales closes, about managing my time, about believing in myself. But I didn't find one book that described how to sell professional services or how to actually run a professional services business and manage the money during and between projects. Unfortunately I had to learn all of the most critical issues to being successfully self-employed on the job.

I pulled out of that slump, and things started to go the way I originally expected. Then I noticed that a lot of people were asking me what I did to get business. They wanted to know how I found work when there wasn't much to be found and how I managed so many projects myself when business was good for everyone. It was only after being part of a panel for a seminar on winning bids that I realized I had a step-by-step process for finding work, doing it and managing my money in between. It was a process for being successfully self-employed.

This book illustrates proven techniques that will help you sell your professional skills. The information will help you establish a solid client base and earn an income greater than you ever could have earned by working for a steady paycheck. It describes the really important process of finding prospects and turning them into clients. It also discusses the nitty gritty of setting up an office in the home. It even takes the mystery out of establishing credit for your business when your business has no credit history.

You won't find 300 successful closes for salespeople in this book, though anyone who sells to earn a living could use the skills outlined. And this book isn't meant to be inspirational, though some of the techniques described in it will inspire you to grow personally as you develop your professional relationships.

The book is anecdotal, based on my own experiences and on the experiences of friends and colleagues who are also self-employed. Best of all, the information in this book will help you build a business that you may never have dreamed possible. Just like I did.

I built a client list that includes companies like Hewlett-Packard, Apple Computer, Mervyn's Stores, and Paramount and government agencies like the Army Corps of Engineers and the United States Coast Guard. And I still do projects for Bank of America. I have directed a series that aired nationally on PBS. I have begun producing and directing another series, and I am developing a CD-ROM title. I have worked throughout North America, Australia and Asia.

Whether you choose self-employment or your former employer forced self-employment on you as part of a company-wide layoff, this book will help you launch and run your business. If your business started well or is slumping, if you need to get business *right now* or just want more business, if you are looking to benefit from someone else's experiential advice or need a reference to help you fine-tune parts of your business, this book is for you. You can use it as a road map to follow so that you, too, can be successfully self-employed.

Acknowledgments

Success is measured in microns of movement toward your own goals. I used to erroneously think that success arrived like the grand prize check from the Publishers Clearing House with television cameras rolling at halftime of the Super Bowl. I have also learned that, though you will make no headway unless you exert your own effort, to succeed you need support in a variety of ways from a variety of people. The process of writing and selling this book, along with over a decade of being self-employed taught me that.

Besides my wife, Donna, there have been a handful of people over the years who have been very supportive of my efforts. In the book I talk about my "Board of Directors," really my advisers. Their counsel, lessons I learned from watching them or listening to them and simply being able to turn to them when I was struggling has made being self-employed easier and more fun. They are all friends, and I thank them for their help in whatever I have achieved.

Mike Alves, an advertising copywriter, knows me well enough to tell me when he thinks I have set a bad course. It is critical to have a good navigator when you pass by rocky shoals. Mike also guided and encouraged me in the early development of this book.

Pete Dickson, an equities trader, and I have rafted down river-cut valleys and hiked over peaks for over 20 years. The views from the peaks have been panoramic, but rides down the rapids have been exhilarating.

Curt Hamm, a contractor, gave me the most critical lesson in selling: "Ask for the business!" He also taught me that you can't hit any target unless you keep your head still during your backswing.

Harry Dorsey, a director of commercials, has been a role model and a mentor since we first worked together in 1981. All of us can learn much from a tour of duty as an apprentice with masters like him.

Ron Sardisco, a banking executive, was an internal corporate client who became a friend. He has a "master's degree" in people skills. Ron gave me some sage counsel early on about clients and about myself. Without that advice, I might have gone back to working for somebody else.

Finally, this book would have never seen print without my agent, Sheree Bykofsky, and her editor, Janet Rosen. Their patience with a novice helped me overcome some significant odds. They have made this process fun, and I appreciate them for that.

CHAPTER 1

Making the Decision To Be Successfully Self-Employed

Scenario One—The Decision Is Made for You

Corporate downsizing . . . rightsizing . . . reengineering—all are euphemisms for layoffs in companies of all sizes across America. Searching for ways to cut overhead and increase returns, companies often choose to reduce staff.

It is no secret that these companies look to cut in areas that have no apparent positive effect on the bottom line. For people who work in areas like communications, training or law—cost centers that are not involved in the "business of the business"—a newspaper headline about 200 people being laid off at Widget Manufacturing just down the road should bring a chill. Of course, it will never happen at International Industries where you work. But things do have a way of going awry.

Here's Your Hat. What's Your Hurry?

Your company announces the sixth straight quarter of disappointing earnings. Within the month, the company president gets the heave-ho from 30,000 feet with a golden parachute that

1

would sink the Bismarck. A week later, an internal announcement about the need to cut back floats across everyone's desks.

Effective immediately, travel to conventions and trade shows is cut, and hiring is frozen along with pending salary increases. Rumors run rampant. People are keeping their fingers crossed, but you hear from one of the guys in manufacturing who heard from his friend in accounting that 70 people will be laid off. Management insists that if everyone simply tightens their departmental belts things will be fine.

Then, one Friday morning your supervisor slips into your office. "Staff meeting in 15 minutes." You check your day planner. "But I didn't hear anything. . ." "I just did," she counters. You notice that she looks paler than usual. "I'll be back to walk you to the meeting." Before you can ask what the meeting is about, she leaves.

It doesn't really hit you between the eyes until some "suit" from personnel is standing in the front of the conference room explaining the severance package the company is offering. "That's it?" you ask yourself. "I'm outta here? What am I gonna do? I'm a trainer, for god's sake."

You don't really get any time to think about anything, but you do have half an hour to clean out your desk. Then it's over.

Besides your Rolodex file, pictures of your family and the two miniature pewter cups the company gave you as a five-year anniversary gift, you carry three month's salary and the cash equivalent of what is left of your vacation out to the parking lot. The toughest choice now is whether to call your spouse with the bad news or head over to the Surf-N-Suds to commiserate with the other people you used to work with. You compromise and decide to call your spouse from the Surf-N-Suds.

As you drive out of the parking lot for the last time, you begin thinking about the things you have been wanting to do besides work for International Industries. You have always wondered what it would be like to be your own boss. You've approved the invoices for vendors who have worked for you. They make three times the money you make, and they get to come and go as they please. You can do that. In fact, you *want* to do that. After all, this is America, home of the free and land of umpteen million brave small businesses owners.

Scenario Two—You Choose Your Own Departure Date

The mass of men lead lives of quiet desperation.

Thoreau

After more than ten years of working for a major bank, not only did that epitaph ache as a yoke on me, I saw others in my graveyard who wore it as well. I sought to grow within the company, but it had just lost a billion dollars for the second year in a row. I was feeling root bound, and the pot was not going to get bigger.

After all, I was not part of the "business of the business," a group that contributed directly to the bottom line. As a producer/director of the company's internal video communications, I provided the company a professional service that, because I was on staff, was cost-effective for them. I liked what I did, and I was willing to adapt within the company—to a degree. I was not interested in becoming part of the business of the business, and the company held a similar view of me.

My department manager arranged for me to speak with the division's senior vice-president about directions I could take within the company. My position gave me lots of project management experience that brought me in contact with a broad spectrum of the organization's senior management. I felt I had something to offer!

Except that there was a hiring freeze, and the senior vice-president did not want to lose the position I occupied. "You're valuable to us where you are," he told me. "There may be an opportunity down the road to move to the position above you."

Right! Le fromage grand never even remembered my immediate supervisor's name. How was my boss ever going to get promoted so that I could? After that meeting, I felt like I had been hobbled. On top of that, corporate policies seemed to be getting more and more ridiculous as losses mounted. I knew I wasn't going anywhere.

The Judge Didn't Sentence You To Work There

Then, one day something popped inside me. The catalyst was another goofball policy issued from above. I screamed to myself, "This gawdforsaken place is NUTS!"

When I stormed in the front door that evening my wife asked generously what was up. "ME!" I screamed. "You know what they did to *me* today?" As we walked through the fields near our house and watched our dogs chase rabbits out of their comfy hutches, my wife listened as I let off steam. I finally ran out of fire, and it got quiet enough to hear the dogs panting 30 yards away. She responded calmly, "You know, the judge didn't sentence you to work there."

The clouds parted and a beam of sunshine poured down on us. What a revelation! The judge *didn't* sentence me to work there. But there is one really crazy thing about this scenario: As important as the revelation was, I can't remember the corporate silliness that set me off that day.

The point? The corporate policy that was my catalyst was actually a minuscule pebble in the shoe of my life. Somehow, though, it got enough of my attention to get me to start planning to take a different path from the one on which I had set out.

The Pros and Cons of Self-Employment

Whether someone plays *Aloha* on the steel guitar for you or whether you sing the song yourself, it is okay not to work for the comfort of a paycheck twice a month. The reality, however, is that working for yourself can be a scary thing. The good news is the shivers that come from being self-employed keep a lot of people who aren't quite as bold from competing with you. And unless you invent something in your garage that will cure cancer, you can expect to work harder for yourself than you ever worked for International Industries.

If you have channel-surfed past infomercials that brag how working for yourself is the way to get control of your own time, keep surfing, dude. When you are on your own and your clients want something from you, you better hop.

Self-Employment's Essence

Ruth Zimmer Boggs, formerly a translator for the German Embassy in Washington, DC, described the essence of being self-employed:

"What surprised me, good of course, was the amount of money I made as a consultant. I was really not prepared for that. I didn't know that kind of money was out there.

"The bad—and I knew that ahead of time—is that there are no guarantees. You have to get out there. You have to drum up business. It's not like you have your paycheck at the end of the month and you can plan on it. You have to have a reserve. You have to be able to survive for a while."

But hopping well and at different speeds for different clients means you get to bill people for all of that hopping. When I worked for the corporation, I got paid a fixed amount regardless of the hopping I did for them. After all, the market dictated that my hopping was only worth so much to them.

Of course, if you can increase the number of people to hop for, you can increase your income. To do that, you have to leave the comfort and apparent security of those paychecks that wrap around you briefly every two weeks. That means risking that you might not get any check for a while. Or worse, that you actually do the work, incur the expenses, and not get any check—*ever*.

Besides selling your professional skills, being on your own means you have to manage your own business. That includes spending time on things like finding health insurance after your COBRA plan expires, preparing for and investing in your retirement, buying and maintaining the right office equipment to help you do your job, understanding and complying with the miasma of government regulations as they affect you and your business, staying on top of the changes within your industry and much more—like actually *doing* your business. If you get the feeling that being in business for yourself can be as lonely

---

Being on Your Own Means:

- Getting health insurance
- Planning and investing in your retirement
- Finding, buying and maintaining the right office equipment
- Understanding and complying with government regulations
- Staying on top of industry changes
- Selling your skills
- Actually doing the work you successfully sold

---

as Gary Cooper looked when he was walking down the middle of the street in *High Noon*, you're not far from wrong.

Given all of that, for some people "quietly desperate" is a good choice. Thanks to my wife and some forgettable corporate policy, I realized it wasn't a choice for me. That you're reading this now indicates that "quietly desperate" probably isn't your choice either.

After that beatific moment in the field, my wife and I began planning a business that would deliver visual communications to Fortune 500 companies. The job would be exactly like the one I did for the company that employed me. I would simply have more than one client.

And I had a distinct advantage; a bright, savvy wife who was and is very supportive. Fortunately, I also had time to plan.

The result?

In my first year of business, I earned more money than I did when I was on staff the year before. Since then, I have grown the business to generate well over $300,000 per year in gross sales and well over $100,000 per year in net income for me and my family. My opportunities continue to expand, as well. I've directed a series that aired on PBS, developed and produced another series of specialty videos, and had a hand in creating a CD-ROM game.

How did I do it? Read on. After all, that's what this book is about.

Learn Through Trial and Error—Yours or Mine

Just after we began planning the business, there was a National Geographic special on PBS about a pride of lions in the African veldt. Typically, lionesses do most of the hunting, but the dominant male gets to feed first after the kill. The lionesses and the rest of the brood chow down after the head of the pride gorges himself. Also typically, when a male lion matures he is forced out of the pride by the dominant male.

This is the most critical time in that young lion's life. Because the lionesses hunt for dinner, the cub does not work very hard for his food—until he is no longer part of the pride. Then it becomes a matter of life and death. He either figures out how to hunt and kill or he weakens from hunger and is killed himself by another animal in the intolerant, unforgiving, unsympathetic African veldt.

The film documented that very challenge faced by one young lion. It was nip and tuck for a while, but after enough trial and error chasing down a variety of animals in a variety of herds, the young lion finally figured out how to get dinner before he became dinner. He went on to form his own pride and got his own lionesses to do the work for him.

As I watched the program, it dawned on me that going into business for myself would be an experience similar to the young lion's. I knew how to apply my professional skills. The question was, would I be able to convince enough people to hire me soon enough to keep me and my family from starving. Like the lion did as a hunter, I was only going to learn how to get business through trial and error.

Not only did I survive, I succeeded. Looking back, my success came because I could do three things. I could sell what I did, I could do what I sold, and I could manage my money between successful projects.

You can too. I discovered that none of it is complicated. In fact, it's all very simple. But don't confuse simple with easy. Being in business for yourself is like starting an exercise program to lose weight. To be effective, it's a slow and steady process of hard work. But if you stick with it, the results will please and amaze you.

You Can Succeed!

- Sell what you do.
- Do what you sell.
- Manage your money in between.

Who Needs To Sell?

You may be thinking, "I don't need to sell. After all, I have never had to sell before." That's because you were on staff, and people within your company probably had to use you. Some professionals genuinely believe that selling is something they won't do and don't need to do. In fact, a role model and mentor of mine said to me once, "I don't peddle." We disagree on that one. You do need to peddle because one way or another you need to reach out to people who can hire you in order to convince them that they should hire you instead of someone else.

"But I have a reputation," you say. "Clients will come to me." Maybe. Then again, maybe there really is a tooth fairy, too.

Clients can come and go through no fault of yours. They get promoted. They retire. They quit to raise a family. They change careers. The corporation gets bought out, and the job function moves across the country under someone else's purview. At some point on your own you will need to go get clients.

Marketing versus Selling

One other thing: Do not confuse "marketing" with "selling." I have heard many self-employed people say, "Business is slow, I better do some marketing." Wrong! They should always be marketing. If business is slow—even if business is brisk—they better do some *selling*.

Marketing is what you do between sales calls. Marketing is determining and describing the focus of your business and what makes you different from your competitors. Marketing is the many steps you take to get your name and expertise in front of prospects and clients so that you can talk to them and they will listen when you are selling. Marketing is sending out press releases to trade magazines and local business publications. Marketing is writing and distributing a newsletter to clients, prospects and others who can feed you work. Marketing is designing and writing your brochure and building an effective mailing list of people who will receive that brochure.

Selling, on the other hand, is *the* final step everyone must take to get the work. Selling is when you ask for the business.

So, if you are facing a beer bust at the Surf-N-Suds or if you choose to be in business for yourself, you are going to have to sell. By following the steps outlined in this book you can achieve the same results I have. You already know your business. You may not know much about how to sell the skills that you have. This book will help you do that. That way, unlike the lion or me who had to learn by trial and error, you can learn to survive— even thrive—from someone who has already been there and done that.

First Step: Learn with Others Who Are on Their Own

If, as I did, you have the advantage of planning your business before you start it, or even if you start your business after you leave the Surf-N-Suds parking lot, talk with people who are already on their own. As important, find people who were on their own but were not successful and talk with them about their experiences. It is much easier on you to learn from other people's experiences than to stumble through the process on your own.

Talk to those self-employed vendors with whom you have a strong relationship. Find out what they did and continue to do to succeed. Be frank and let them know that you are considering going out on your own. They will appreciate knowing your plans because they will need to develop another client to fill in the business they might lose when you leave. They may also give you some leads.

> ### Learn from Others
>
> * Your current vendors
> * SCORE
> * Others who have run or are running
>   a business
> * Local community college

Service Corps of Retired Executives, known as SCORE, often holds seminars for those who are starting out on their own. Attend those seminars to gain advice.

Look around you for others who can tell you about running a small business. For example, when we were planning the business, my wife was the Senior Vice-President of Lending at a very large credit union. One of her daily duties was interviewing marginal loan candidates to decide whether or not the credit union should lend them money. She talked with many people who were self-employed and others who went or seemed to be going bankrupt. Through her interviews and conversations with those marginal loan candidates we learned a lot about what to do and what not to do.

Finally, many community colleges offer refresher or basic business courses. You can glean a lot of information from them about writing business plans, marketing and more. Take advantage of them. In fact, many of the vendors I work with still participate in some periodic continuing education business classes.

How To Use This Book

One thing about this book and how you use it: I wrote this from the perspective of one who has primarily produced corporate video programs. If you used to work in the public relations department for International Industries or in management information services or training or legal, you should find it easy to adapt some of my advice to your particular expertise and to your own personality.

As my cousin said to me when I told him about our plan to start a business, "The difference between those who do and those who don't are those who start." So, let's get rolling.

CHAPTER 2

Selling and What Keeps Us from It

To succeed on your own you have to sell what you do, do what you sell and then manage the money in between success-ful projects. "But I don't know how to sell," you say. You also didn't know about law or training or video production when you started either. So you learned. You can learn how to sell. I did.

I am not a born salesman. In fact, before I went out on my own, the sum total of my sales experience was two years of occasionally working behind the jewelry counter at a K-Mart during high school. I also produced and directed several sales training videos for my former employer, absorbing some infor-mation by osmosis. So, just like everyone else who has ever sold, I had to learn how to sell.

Many People Have a Negative Perception of Salespeople

The problem many people have with selling is their own *perception* of salespeople. They see anyone who sells as another Herb Tarlick, the randy, loudly dressed salesman in the television series *WKRP in Cincinnati*. No one consciously wants to be seen like old Herb.

But stop and think about this for a moment. Companies are cutting back in areas like the one in which you specialize. They hire people like you and me to do specific jobs in a specific amount of time and then expect us to go away. Companies need us because they have been getting rid of us by the millions. A friend and colleague who works with me calls us the new generation of employees. The work within these companies still needs to be done even though there is no longer the staff to do it. It is up to us to ask for the business. We are not selling cars or vacuum cleaners. We are selling support relationships. We are part of this new, virtual corporation.

People Also Overcomplicate Selling

I also believe that people overcomplicate selling. You can read books on a myriad of sure-fire closes, but those closes don't help you initiate the relationship. They also don't help you do the work you have been hired to do. Finally, books like that don't help you maintain the relationship once you get things rolling with your client.

Besides overcomplicating selling, people have two great fears that keep them from selling: Fear of rejection and fear of failure.

Fear of Rejection

Every morning when we wake up, we want people to like us. Because our business relationships are based on personal relationships, it is easy to confuse asking people for the business with asking them if they like us. To an extent, they must like us to want to buy from us. It is understandable that we don't want to put ourselves in a position to have people tell us they don't like us. To succeed, however, you have to get past that. To get past that, consider that you are building relationships—not selling one car one time to one person and then never seeing that person again.

How To Overcome Fear of Rejection

Try to approach the selling process as someone who is part of the new generation of employees. You are simply offering to help. Companies need your help because they are thinning their ranks of people like us all of the time. Ask anybody who is still at International Industries and they will tell you that the work load hasn't lessened because there are fewer people on staff. More and more people who are still on staff have their own pager, cellular phone, laptop computer and fax at home just to try to keep up with the work load for fear of ending up out of work, too. You just have to tell your story to people who need you to help them lighten their work load.

The trick is to find them—which we talk about later. There are lots of people who need your help, but their companies won't let them hire outsiders. Other companies won't approve the budgets to pay you what you want to work for. Obviously you need to qualify the prospects you call on, but because you won't absolutely know what goes on behind all of those palace walls, you will call on many people who can't use you or won't be able to afford you. You're also going to call on people who really don't need you.

If a prospect turns you down, consider that you aren't personally being rejected. You were probably turned down because that person just doesn't need or want the services you offered.

It's Really about Making Positive Impressions

The process of building your business becomes a matter of number of impressions on the people who can afford you, who want to hire you and whose company needs your skills.

In order to get us to buy their products, Proctor & Gamble spends millions of dollars every year flooding us with advertising about those products. Generally, the ones that stick in our minds do so after we see an advertisement for a product about a squizillion times. Proctor & Gamble runs ads as often as possible in order to create as many impressions on us as possible. They have built a business by expecting that when we have to choose, we'll choose Procter & Gamble products because we are humming the jingles while we walk down the supermarket aisles.

Look at it another way. Pete Rose now holds major league baseball's record for most hits in a career. He surpassed Ty Cobb's record that stood for years. But Rose's lifetime batting average isn't better than Cobb's. There is no questioning Pete Rose's greatness as a baseball player, but one of the reasons he broke Cobb's record is because he stepped up to the plate more than Ty Cobb did.

In terms of my own selling, I know there are hundreds of businesses in the San Francisco Bay Area that need visual communications projects produced. When I started on my own I knew that if I called on enough businesses, sooner or later I could convince at least one to let me produce a video project for them. I also knew that if I did the work the way they expected it to be done, sooner or later, they would ask me back to do more projects for them. Then, based on my experience with that company, I could get another company to hire me. With the experience of having worked independently for two companies, a third would be more inclined to have me work for them—and so on.

Overcome fear of rejection by realizing that not every company will be able to afford what you do, want what you do or need what you do. Get to the plate often, and you will be able to generate a client base that ultimately will allow you to not have to sell to a new prospect every single day. The more prospects you contact when you begin your business, the sooner you will find the clients you need to provide the foundation on which you will build a successful business.

Fear of Failure

You may still be reticent to ask for the business because you think that if the prospect says "no" that you are a failure. If you are selling a relationship, the prospect may turn you down simply because she is not in the market for your skills or may already have enough vendors who do what you do.

If the prospect turns you down after you have carefully listened to what she wants and needs, and if you have properly presented your story based on what you heard, then you can be certain that she truly is not interested in your help. On the other hand, if you did not listen carefully to understand the client's wants and needs, and you did not present your story carefully, then you did fail.

How can you tell the difference? When you work for yourself, a little voice inside you will let you know when you didn't do everything that you could. So take the experience as a step toward learning how to sell and how to do better next time at the plate.

The sales process for people who deliver on-going professional services is a mechanical one. Once you establish a relationship with a client, you only have to nurture the relationship. Of course, a key element to that nurturing is continuing to look for ways to meet that client's needs.

Two Kinds of Selling

There are two different kinds of selling. You can be an order-taker or an order-maker. Being an order-taker is when people call you up and say, "Hey—I've got this work that needs to be done. Are you available?" You are an order-maker when you are familiar enough with your client's business to propose projects to them.

There is nothing wrong with order-taking. I have picked up lots of projects along the way because I was around when the client was looking to dish the work off on a vendor. During casual conversation, a client might mention a need for an upcoming project. I always offer to help. More often than not, the client is glad to get that project off the "To Do" list.

Order-making has a couple of benefits. One is that, because you are knowledgeable enough to propose the project, you are probably the best vendor to do it. If the client decides to go ahead with the project, you will probably get the nod to do it, too. The second benefit is that, even if the client nixes the project, you have tried to help the client. You have exhibited interest in her business. That can go a long, long way for you.

It might not bring you a paycheck that one time, but it will certainly give you an inside track on future projects.

Remember the adage, "The easiest prospect to land is the client you already have." Once you establish a client relationship with someone take care of that relationship. Nurture it. In turn the client will take care of you.

Once You Start Selling, Don't Stop!

Once you have established your client base, you won't have the daily task of selling to a bunch of new prospects. But don't ever forget that clients have a way of fading with the sunset. That means that you should always have a business development plan working.

I learned that valuable information early on from one of my scriptwriters. He is a talented guy who works in the advertising business as a freelance photographer and copywriter.

One day he called me, looking for leads. Since I perceived him as somebody who worked regularly, I was surprised and asked him why he needed leads. It turned out that all of his clients had evaporated. One had been relocated, another had been laid off, another quit and two others were with businesses that were moved out of state when the companies got bought out. All of this happened within a month, and my friend was now looking to establish a new client base.

That was an object lesson for me. From then on I made sure that I did everything I could to keep the flow of clients fresh. Unfortunately for my friend, he still hasn't learned from his own experience. In the ensuing six years, I received two similar calls from him.

Mark Twain said, "Put all of your eggs in one basket, then watch that basket!" Some people in my business who work independently are comfortable with only two or three clients. Some even have just one. I believe it's in my own best interest to have several clients because the market is always changing. I weathered a pretty significant recession because I had a wide range of clients. Some of my competitors didn't fair as well.

I played football when I was in college. My head coach had a sign over his desk. It read, "Recruiting is like shaving, if you miss a day, you look like a bum." When it comes to getting young athletes to attend a certain college, recruiting is selling. Like my old coach, you need to keep selling. Fortunately, you don't need 20 or 30 new freshmen every year. But you should constantly look for ways to help your current clients. Also keep looking for new clients when you have the chance.

The best way to start and continue to look for new clients is to have a business plan.

CHAPTER 3

Creating Your Business Plan and Finding Clients

Whether you have a year to plan before launching your business, or if you design your logo on a Surf-N-Suds napkin, you probably have certain expectations about how long it will take to really get rolling. Regardless of the business you are in, you must give yourself some time. My brother retired from a career as a Navy pilot and started another career in real estate. It took him two years to fill the pipeline with sellers and buyers. Another person I know opened a restaurant, and it was also about two years before he could start taking any significant amount of money out of the business.

Selling professional services is the same. A very few people may be successful right away. Others may take longer. Some people may not have much time.

Just Starting Out? Then Be Frugal

Of course, if you dive right in to the waters of self-employment after the wake at Surf-N-Suds, you need to start swimming right away. Apply the techniques in this book, and you have a very good chance of surviving—even thriving.

The first thing to do? Quit spending money on the frivolous or purely pleasurable. Be frugal. If you persevere, if you are diligent, if you are disciplined, you'll find soon enough that you are making more money than when you worked at International Industries. Expect to take at least two years to really get rolling and you won't be disappointed.

In late summer of 1991 a friend and colleague who competed with me for the same business had a heart attack. It became obvious to him that he needed to change not only his lifestyle, but also—to try to reduce stress—the way he earned a living. He foresaw an evolution in our industry—more powerful, less expensive computers were making basic video editing systems more powerful and less expensive. So he invested in his vision and set up a boutique video editing facility targeted at professionals like me. It took him until early 1994—over two years—to complete the transition. By then his facility was booked nearly every day, and he was able to enjoy a two-week trip to Europe with his wife.

Businesses Fail for Three Reasons

1. Poor planning
2. Not enough money
3. Too much overhead

Good Planning and No Overhead Overcomes No Money

Planning for a two-year start-up means having enough cash and credit to get you through the toughest period. A combination of poor planning, not enough money and excessive overhead cause most businesses to fail in their early days. If you plan well, and if you keep your overhead down, not having enough money becomes less of a liability. Having enough money gives you the luxury of more time to get things rolling.

Speaking of time, when I went on my own I believed my channel-surfing eyes that going into business for myself would give me a lot more time off. I actually expected to lower my golf score and take flying lessons while I built my business. I was surprised.

I shouldn't have been, because the equation is so simple. No work equals no income. No income means that I can't pay the mortgage.

On my own, I have worked harder than I ever did for any company that employed me. If I spend an entire work week on a project, I still have to keep an eye on the future by generating more business and accomplishing other tasks that I can't bill for—though they are as important.

You Can't Always Play When You Want

I try to take a long Thanksgiving weekend off every year to drive to the mountains to get a Christmas tree with my family. A trip like that really kicks off the holiday season for us, and it's something we always look forward to.

Around Thanksgiving in 1994, I had three projects waxing or waning and one that was as full as the harvest moon. I was about as busy as a 24-hour clock will let a person be. The project I just finished had taken a couple of 80-hour weeks. Invoices from vendors were coming in, and I needed to close out the books on that job. But I was running 12-hour days on the current project, coordinating the two projects that would follow, negotiating a CD-ROM game contract and working on this book. In fact, to get everything done, I had to work the Friday and Monday following Thanksgiving instead of going to the mountains. I was struggling to keep the weekend open to enjoy with my family and friends.

The irony was that I was only going to be busy through the end of the year. January and beyond was as wide open as the great American West. That is, until late Friday afternoon when I received a call from someone in a company that I had been trying to add to my client list.

He needed a project completed by mid-January and wanted to know if I could develop a treatment, project plan and budget by the following Tuesday. I told him that I could. I thought to myself, however, that I didn't know *when* I could do it. In theory, I have a life outside of my profession, but I need to keep the pipeline full, too, and I have to attend to the details of my business—like paying vendors.

The following Saturday morning we planned to get our tree. Saturday afternoon we were off to a wedding of my wife's lifelong friend. My wife's sister was in town Saturday evening, so we'd be going to a family dinner. Sunday's schedule wasn't much different. I also knew that the following week would continue with 12-hour days on the current project.

So, on Saturday morning I got up hours before anybody else in the house to accomplish several things. I spent about three hours dealing with money, paying invoices from vendors who worked on the just-completed project, balancing the books and so on. Another hour was spent reviewing my business insurance policies. I was trying desperately to keep that expense category down, and I was comparing my standing policies with those offered through a trade organization. Of course, I also needed to get the proposal developed. I didn't complete everything I wanted to do, but I knocked a lot of tasks off of my list.

If I planned to work in January, I still had to get that proposal completed. But when?

Very early Monday morning the alarm went off. I spent three hours writing the treatment and an hour running numbers. Then I printed a draft of the proposal and reviewed it throughout the day when opportunities to do that arose.

That night, after the house got quiet, I printed up the final proposal, and the next morning on the way to an edit session I got it bound. When we broke for lunch, I presented the proposal to my client, and the wheels were set in motion to complete the brand new project by mid-January.

Of course, my schedule isn't always as full as the scenario I just gave, but I usually do work at least a 60-hour week. That's time spent doing the work, time spent getting the work and time spent managing the business. It's hard to give a precise ratio of time spent doing those three things, but on average about 20 to 25 percent of the work week is spent getting new work and managing the business. In other words, maybe one day a week is spent on non-billable work.

Being in business for yourself means making many choices. One is choosing between work and play. You can't always play when you want to or you can choose to work less frequently. We're all different, and I don't believe anyone is willing to spend 80 hours, 52 weeks out of the year on work. I know I don't. Though that was a hectic time for me, I had also taken six weeks of vacation that year.

Would I have still gone out on my own if I really knew how hard I would work? Absolutely. In fact, the early days of self-employment were nearly euphoric. There were no more daily commuting hassles, endless staff meetings or silly policies to follow. In the afternoons in town as the commuter bus passed me I thought to myself, "There but for the grace of God. . ." I was on my own. When I wasn't developing business, I spent time setting up my back-office operations.

Turning the First Plan into Action

I got my first call from a big high-technology company in the Silicon Valley at the end of February, less than a month after I hung my shingle out, and things started to roll. One project seemed to lead to another. In June, I confidently told my wife that we could expect to be earning $10,000 a month, net, within the year.

The business plan my wife and I wrote before we started the business was working, but by the end of the first year we still hadn't regularly reached the $10,000 monthly net income that I expected. Into the late summer of the second year, business was still growing well enough to give us the confidence to have a new home built. However, it seemed that I was still doing a lot of selling of what I did, and not a lot of doing of what I sold. By the end of the year, business really dropped off. The quarter before we moved into our new home, I netted $27. I don't know what your house payments are, but it'd be tough making them on $9 per month.

Two things were happening. First, I was running out of prospects on whom to call. It was really starting to feel like an exercise program. Because it was feeling like a grind, I also started finding reasons not to call on the prospects I had already contacted.

My early successes led me to believe that being on my own would be as easy as working for my old company. At first it was. I bounded out of bed every morning looking to hook a new client. As time wore on, though, I wasn't quite so spry. In fact, I had periodic inclinations to throw in the towel.

Finally, I did what athletes do when they slump. I went back to the basics—the basic goals and targets I described in the business plan that we wrote before I went out on my own.

The Business Plan Gives You Something To Shoot For

If you golf, you know that most driving ranges have flags as targets at various regular distances. Otherwise, without the flags you'd just be hitting toward some imagined point, getting only a vague idea of your accuracy. And in golf, accuracy is everything!

One sunny Saturday morning a friend and I were warming up for a round by hitting a few balls at the driving range. This particular range was only a vast expanse of green—no target flags were up that morning. Neither of us seemed to give it much thought, because we were simply enjoying each other's company and practicing our swings.

My swing was something else that morning. I mean, the ball was jumping off of the club. My friend commented on the distance I was getting, and I'd be lying if I said the distance didn't impress me, too. In fact, when the starter called our names, I practically ran to the first tee.

Well, the first fairway was a lot different than the vast expanse of driving range where we warmed up. Trees lined both sides of the length of the fairway. Sand traps were also placed strategically out there as well. Fortunately, the trees and the sand traps didn't come into play for me, because I really—and I do mean really—hit a monster drive. In truth, however, the hazards of the first fairway didn't come into play because my ball landed in the fairway next to us.

The point? In business as in golf, if you want to know how well you are shooting, you need to aim at a target. A business

---

A Plan Is Also Something To Reflect Upon

When I went back to review my business plan during that slump, I realized that I needed even more prospects to call on than I originally anticipated. So I set about to increase the prospect list. As naive as the initial plan was, it allowed me to review my situation and begin to rectify it.

---

plan is the target, and it also describes *how* you will hit the target.

Writing a Plan To Adapt or Migrate—Not Perish

Zoologists and anthropologists say that for a species to survive it must adapt or migrate, otherwise it will perish. A business plan helps you to adapt or migrate.

Consider this. You want to go on a vacation. First, decide on a destination, say Yellowstone National Park. Then decide how you're going to get there—the mode of travel, the route you'll take, how much time you will spend getting there and so on.

The business plan does the same thing. By writing it, you are forced to describe where you want to go. Then you have to think through and describe how you'll get there.

As with driving to Yellowstone, knowing how you want to get someplace gives you the flexibility to change your route along the way. If you know how long it will take or how much it will cost to do something, you'll know whether the change is necessary or worthwhile. Also, if you get lost or sidetracked, you can pull out your map, aka Business Plan, and review how to get back on course.

My original business plan seems naive when I look at it now (see page 38). It certainly was simple. Simple is almost always better. You don't need to make brain surgery out of writing your plan as long as you do write it.

What Goes into a Good Plan

Then if my plan was so naive, how come it worked? It worked because the plan had specifics. It included clearly defined goals with achievable deadlines, and the results we wanted to achieve were measurable ones. For example, my most important goal was to get business.

The plan might have read, "Get business—fast." Though I needed to contact prospects such a sentence would be of little help. Instead, I wrote, "Contact at least three prospects every day until the flow of business impedes effectively calling."

A bad plan might say something high falutin like, "We seek to be the premier provider of accounting computer programming in the United States." Great concept. But *what steps* are necessary to become the premier provider? Who is the premier provider currently, and why? What will you need to do to be considered one of the best? How long do you plan to take to become the best? Is that time frame realistic? Do you need to build a staff, change locations, or can you do it all on your own? What industry changes might prevent you from achieving that goal, and how might you overcome those obstacles?

Elements of a Good Plan

- Clearly defined goals
- Step-by-step descriptions of how to reach them
- Achievable deadlines
- Measurable results

I should have been more definitive with my plan. I should have described what I meant by "impedes effectively calling." In my mind it meant that I would be doing so much work that I couldn't break away from the project with which I was currently involved.

Setting Objectives

What else was in my original business plan? To begin with, I listed our objectives, the "destinations" or things we believed I needed to accomplish within six months, one year and five years after starting the business. Doing that helped me to think through the market, consider how I would enter it and anticipate the market's evolution as well.

Targeting Industries, Then Companies Within Those Industries

Next, I identified industries to sell to. Generally, people find it easier to hire you if you have done some work in their industry. It's easier to bring you up to speed, and you can probably speak some of their jargon. Also it helps to build a relationship if you've already done something in your prospect's industry.

My experience in the financial services industry made banks, savings and loans, and credit unions obvious targets. I had done some freelance work for one of the largest high-tech firms in Silicon Valley. That made the high-tech industry another obvious choice.

When we were writing the plan, a minimum budget for a solid corporate video production was $20,000. Projects generally ran around $40,000. Obviously, my prospects had to be able to afford such a project.

When I target prospects, I use a couple of rules of thumb to qualify them—to ensure that calling on them is worth my time and theirs. One rule is that the featured product in a sales videotape needs to generate at least $5 million in annual sales to justify the project's expense. Another rule is that a company should be large enough to have someone in charge of training. If so, the company might want customized training videotapes. Generally, those companies are at least $100 million in size.

Lots of reading and other research lead me to establish those rules of thumb. Obviously, the cost of a videotape—along with many other internal costs—is supported by the product's sales. Products that generate less than $5 million in sales just do not throw off enough money to warrant producing a videotape. Companies under $100 million in size generally do not have enough employees to need training materials that can't be bought off the shelf. On top of that, those businesses very likely don't have a lot of branch offices with similar positions that necessitate everyone learning exactly the same things.

Increase Your Odds for Success!

- Target industries to sell to immediately or in which your skills can be applied right away.
- Make certain prospects can afford your work.
- It helps if target businesses are within your proximity.

Besides meeting those general qualifications, my targets also had to have headquarters or large divisional offices nearby. It usually requires senior level approval for the budget it takes to produce a video. So it helps to be where the work is to get some of it.

Putting Yourself Where the Work Is.   On a family holiday to Australia, we took a sightseeing day-trip on a train. Though the tour company picked us up at our apartment in the morning, we were on our own at the end of the day when we returned to the station. We expected to catch a cab back to our hotel, but there were only a handful of cabs waiting to pick up passengers. Because my wife and I were traveling with a five-month-old and a two-year-old we didn't move fast enough to get one of the cabs. We weren't alone. There were a couple of dozen other people who didn't move quickly enough either. Soon some other cabs pulled up to the station, and we were headed back to the hotel.

I asked the driver why there were so few of his colleagues waiting to pick up fares at the train station. After all, the train arrives every day with passengers who need rides back to their

> ## To Identify and Qualify Prospects, Identify Qualities in Their Businesses that You Want or Need
>
> - How big must the company be? Employees? Gross sales? Net value?
> - How many products should the company carry?
> - Should the company have offices in other parts of the region, state, country or globe?
> - Must the company need or have relationships with other businesses or government agencies?
> - Does the company need to be on the cutting edge of its industry to succeed?

respective hotels. He smiled and said he didn't understand it either. He said that at the end of the day, there were usually drivers who complained that they didn't pick up any fares in the afternoon. Our driver, on the other hand, took advantage of the train's schedule and usually picked up half-a-dozen fares every day from the station. His unsuccessful mates spent their time in cab queues in front of the very hotels which people needed to get to from the train station.

Closer to home, Nordstrom is headquartered in Seattle, Washington. I work out of the San Francisco Bay Area. I'd be wasting my time if I went to the local Nordstrom to try to sell to the company. There are plenty of other companies that are headquartered near me. For my business, I can use my time and resources better by selling to those companies with headquarters nearby.

A Project Can Open a New Niche

Ruth Zimmer Boggs was a translator for the German Embassy in Washington, DC. Her first project as an independent was translating documents from German to English for a major law firm that specializes in patent law.

As a result of her experience with that one project, she contacted all of the other firms in the region that specialize in patent law. She also began to contact other businesses that might need translators—places like publishing houses, television stations, the State Department, the International Monetary Fund and the World Bank.

Determining Your Criteria To Narrow Down Your Prospect List

In the process of writing the plan, I determined that I could increase my odds for success by finding businesses that met three broad criteria.

1. They needed to be either in an industry that I could sell into immediately or in an industry where I could demonstrate an easy transfer of my expertise.
2. They needed to be large enough to afford the kind of work I produced.
3. They also needed to be in the general vicinity of the greater San Francisco Bay Area. To succeed you need to sort out the criteria that businesses you sell to must meet. Writing a plan makes you establish the criteria.

I considered the kinds of industries that might meet these criteria and came up with three other industries to sell into besides financial services and high technology. They were manufacturing, retailing and agriculture. I could easily do video projects on personal benefits, employee orientation and so on, because I had done those types of projects before. Several corporate headquarters in each industry were present in the

---

A Business Plan Can Help Raise Money

Marsha Vdovin used her plan to raise money for her public relations firm. Though she planned for over six months to start the business, she felt like she needed more money than she had saved to get started.

"I didn't have anything for the office. I didn't have a computer. So I felt like I needed to raise money for all of the office equipment and to have a financial cushion," she said.

She went to friends with her plan to raise the money she needed.

"My business plan was more like a financial plan," she said. It had specifics like what she expected to have for billable time, and the rates she would charge.

The Business Plan Also Helped Her Focus

The business plan helped her define the things she would offer in business, what her advantages were and what her experience was.

Even with that perspective, Marsha said she could have gone even further. "I didn't do enough research on who the competition was and their rates."

Bay Area and the surrounding region. Each business we identified could afford our product. Best of all, we had an opportunity with each to create a ripple effect on our client base. For example, if one retailer liked our work, the odds were good that another retailer would too. In that manner I could build my client base, and from that my client list would grow.

Focusing First on Specific Businesses

My plan was to develop at least two clients in each of the five industries I targeted. In my business, a project generally lasts anywhere from one to six weeks. If I could produce two projects for each client in the five industries I targeted, I would be producing about 20 projects per year. Add to that the occasional project for one-shot clients, and I would be able to bill for at least 40 weeks of my time per year. Considering a minimum net of $2,000 per week, I could easily anticipate a net annual income of over $80,000.

Then Focusing on the Buyers in Them

Once I targeted businesses within specific industries, I needed to identify specific *buyers* to sell to. So who were the buyers? Or who could tell me who the buyers were?

Steal a little technique from people who sell insurance. Once they get out of their basic sales training classes, the novitiates are sent after friends and relatives to launch their sales careers. Consider all of the people you know—even barely—to begin building your prospect list. We did that. We also listed people we *thought* could refer us to other people.

How Much Business Do You Need?

I targeted five industries, then two businesses in each industry.

Two projects for each client every year meant I would enjoy a steady flow of work.

A business plan like that will help you as it helped me when things go slower than you like. And when business dropped off in my second year, I referred back to the business plan to brainstorm about other prospects I hadn't considered. Also, I was able to better define my prospect list when I referred back to the plan because I had more selling experience. That experience gave me a better focus to approach business development.

As a result, my business development program picked up and I added a high-tech client and one of the country's largest credit unions. Best of all, I got out of my slump and never looked back.

That's not to say things have always been rosy. As with life, there is an ebb and flow to business. The following year I hit a six-week skid. So I went back to my plan one more time. Doing so, I realized that there was one major bank that I had unsuccessfully approached earlier. My original prospect had moved on within the company, and a new decision-maker was in her place. I began calling on the new prospect in March. My overall business started to increase, and that took me away from a pure selling mode. But my early successful rapport with the new prospect encouraged me to continue calling on her. That September, the prospect became my client, and I produced 17 projects for her over the next 15 months.

Another Creative Way To Build Business

A friend of mine built his advertising agency by producing annual reports for corporations. Working for a small agency, he developed strong experience producing quality annual reports cost-effectively. When he decided to form his own agency he devised a successful strategy.

Just a bit of research helped him generate a long list of companies that he knew would be interested in his ability to produce annual reports. He targeted those companies and, with a stack of his work under his arm, he methodically called on each company on the list. Many of the companies he called on were happy with their agencies. There were enough companies, however, that asked him to produce their annual reports.

Those successes allowed him to build personal relationships with people within those companies. From those relationships business flowed, and his agency grew.

Creating a Plan Based on the Inverted Pyramid

What if you are an accountant who relocated from a major metropolitan area like Dallas to a smaller area like Boise? When you were in Dallas did you work with middle-market companies or did you specialize in franchises? If you worked with middle-market companies, look for those similar to the ones with which you have experience. If you specialized in working with franchises, look for those types of businesses. Then, target specific companies that are most likely to need your expertise, identify the people in those companies who are most likely to hire you and go from there.

Your Business Is Based on Who Your Targets Are

Laurie Girand, a Stanford MBA and former evangelist for Apple Computer, heads Beyond Marketing, a software marketing and strategy firm. She targets venture-funded businesses or well-financed businesses.

"I have worked for the small guys," she said, "and it's excruciating working for them. . . . Not because they don't pay. In fact, sometimes they pay better than the funded guys. They're just not going to bring in the dollar level of business we are looking for."

What if you were the only training professional for Acclimated Manufacturing in Boise when the company laid you and 50 others off? There are actually three directions in which you can go.

First, look for companies which have trainers like you on staff. At the very least, you can help augment the staff when one or more of them takes an extended vacation or maternity leave. You may even be able to offer a specific training program based on the one that you developed when you were at Acclimated Manufacturing.

The Business Plan Makes You Think

Aurelia Cassidy used to work in the Corporate Education Department at Hewlett-Packard. She was responsible for supervising the planning, coordination and management of 40 weeks of training per year at the company's corporate headquarters. Now she plans meetings and coordinates trade shows for a variety of companies.

"I put a structured plan into place because one of these days this is going to take off," she said, "and I am not going to be able to do it all myself. If I am going to end up hiring people, then I have to have a business plan."

What Did She Focus On?

"The different products I have. . . What are the different skills that are saleable? There's the teleconferencing area. There's the trade show area. There's the special events area. Then there's the training area. How are they all compatible and how do they work together?"

"Then I sat down and thought, how am I going to develop each one? Do I need all of them? Am I taking too much on myself or do I have to hire somebody?"

Second, look also for companies that—due to the complexity of tasks in manufacturing or customer service—should have a trainer but don't. Your strength lies in your past work at Acclimated Manufacturing. Determine what kinds of training those companies can and need to buy, then set about convincing them of your abilities to meet their needs.

Third, of course, do not forget your long-established contacts at Acclimated Manufacturing. People there should have grown used to your expertise. Since there is no longer anyone on staff who does what you did for the company, an outsider with strong working knowledge of the company is an ideal candidate for the company to bring in on a project-by-project basis.

Fourth, paint a bulls-eye on each of your targets of opportunity by identifying that person in each company who will hire you to do that voodoo that you do so well. Then, outline a step-by-step approach to convince those people to hire you. Finally, set your plan into motion.

Advice about Finding Work with Your Old Company. Conventional wisdom says that you should try to walk away with a contract from Acclimated Manufacturing—especially if you were laid off in a downsizing move. After all, you probably have half the important names and their phone numbers memorized. Don't be too tempted to rely solely on your former employer. The temptation lies in the ease and comfort of knowing your clients so well. Do get as much work as you can from them, but expand your base as quickly as possible to avoid becoming too dependent on just one client.

In my case, when I left my old company the head of my department made it very clear to me that he resented it when people who went out on their own came back to fat contracts. He told me that he would not hire me for at least one year after my separation date.

That may sound harsh, but he actually did me a favor because I was forced to find and get business from other sources. I built my business with a foundation of new clients. Of course, one year after I left, I took him to lunch to discuss opportunities within his purview, and he is a valued client now.

The First Business Plan

My first business plan seems naive now. You can see for yourself. I have included both the first year's plan and the plan which resulted from the slump.

The first plan gave me a foundation of objectives to work towards. All of it was based on my own tempered projections of how I expected things to go. Many of the vague areas were not so vague in my own mind. When you write your plan try to fill it with as much detail as possible—even if, as I did, you have to project or guesstimate.

You will see there was much more detail in the second plan than there was in the first, mostly because I had some experience to base the plan on. Best of all, going back to review and rewrite the plan gave me a renewal. As a result, business began to build—slowly at first, then it started snowballing. We truly never have looked back.

The following examples are my actual business plans. They may contain technical information about my own business that is confusing to you. The point is to show you how simple a plan can be so that you will write your own and to show you how business—and your plan—can evolve.

Revising a Plan after Gaining Experience

When things started to slump, I went back to my original plan and reviewed it. Having two years of experience being on my own, I was able to enhance the plan with more detail and fewer guesstimates.

BRENNAN & ASSOCIATES' BUSINESS PLAN

SIX-MONTH GOALS

- Establish a functioning office, including:
  - Thorough knowledge of the following computer programs—dBase, DOS, Lotus 1-2-3, WordPerfect and Commando.
  - Install phone system which consists of "call waiting," recording capabilities, speaker phone and message check-in.
  - A letter-quality printer.
  - Establish a call-file of current and potential clients, leads, etc.
  - Purchase high-end VCR/monitor system.
  - Establish internal accounting/billing functions.
- Develop a marketing plan, including:
  - A cover letter, demo tape, research whether yellow page ads are worthwhile.
- Make three contacts per day until project flow impedes contacting potential clients.
  - Our obvious strengths, based on our career with Bank of America and the freelance projects we have written, produced and directed, lie in the financial services industry and in the high-technology industry. Besides those, other potential industries include Retail (several major retailers have headquarters in the Bay Area), Agriculture (particularly wineries), Manufacturing. Identify, target and contact potential clients in each of those industries.
- Potential clients include:
  - CORPORATIONS—Bank of America, Chevron, Hewlett-Packard, Shaklee, Pacific Bell

- AD AGENCIES—Teresa Imel's dad, Grey Advertising and Jim Allen at McAnn-Erickson. Other possible clients include Solem-Loeb Associates, Wineries, FinanceAmerica, AirProducts and contacts through trade organizations.
- Initiate four projects.
- Earn $12,000 before expenses. One bottom line project billed at over $20,000 which nets $8,000, and two fee-based projects which net $2,000 each.

ONE-YEAR PLAN

- Have at least three repeat clients.
- Initiate 16 projects by year-end.
- Earn two referral projects.
- Income to exceed $36,000. Two bottom line projects of over $20,000 which net $8,000 each, and ten fee-based projects which net $2,000 each.
- Buy an off-line editing system.

FIVE-YEAR PLAN

- Manage three projects per month.
- Hire a part-time assistant.
- Buy two acres in Sonoma with a barn for the office.
- Income to exceed $125,000. Five bottom line projects of over $35,000 which net $15,000 each, and ten fee-based projects which net $5,000 each.

BRENNAN/ASSOCIATES' 1989 BUSINESS PLAN

Brennan/Associates' business plan should be considered a road map of our plans for the coming year.

The goals outlined in this business plan are intended to be met at dates throughout the year. If no date is specified, then by December 1989. Still, the plan may be revised or updated quarterly.

Basic Business Purpose:

To maintain financial stability by profitably providing businesses and government agencies with communications programs or parts of communications programs that enhance those entities' abilities to reach specific target groups to inform, motivate, train or advocate the positions, products, services or stature of those entities.

On-Going Objectives:

- Continue to write a business plan annually.
- Review and update the business plan quarterly.
- Maintain a weekly routine managing financial reports.
- Write and send press releases as projects are contracted for or are completed.

Financial Objectives:

The financial goal is to generate $134,000 of gross production revenues, which will result in income of at least $67,000 before taxes.

To achieve that goal, we must:

- Complete nine fee-based projects at an average of $3,000 per project.
- Complete five bottom-line projects with an average production budget of $21,400, the profits of which should average $8,000 per project.

Additional financial objectives include:

- By January 31, 1989, write and establish a financial plan for the personal finances, managing money already set aside for retirement as though the money were its own business.

- Begin setting aside 25% of income from fee-based projects and from profit of bottom-line projects in a savings account to increase cash reserves which can be relied upon in periods of economic recession. Those cash reserves can be either in the form of Certificates of Deposit in a secure bank or credit union, or in the form of Treasury Securities.

Marketing Objectives:

To continue new business development by contacting at least three potential clients every week. This will help establish, then maintain a flow of continuous projects, and reduce the likelihood of a production slump.

We want to expand our client base to include a steady client like Hewlett-Packard from each of the following industries:

- Retail—like Mervyn's, Ross Stores, or Safeway

- Agriculture—like E. & J. Gallo

- Advertising—like McCann-Erickson or Thomas/Rahm

- Securities—like Charles Schwab or the Pacific Stock Exchange

- Industry—like Expo Matik or OCLI

Once we've established a client in a given industry, we will focus on expanding within that particular industry, much like we did in the high-tech industry, growing from Hewlett-Packard to Varian and Tandem Computers, and so on.

Some industries may cross, like ComputerLand, a retailer of high-technology products, which will be beneficial to us. For example, garnering Safeway as a client may result from our work with an agriculture industry client, or vice versa.

The potential clients for whom we can deliver bottom-line related projects are:

Company	Contact
Beauty Store and More	Amy Goodman, President
AutoDesk	Susan Sheridan, VP - Marketing
Charles Schwab	Donna Goldman
Levi Strauss & Company	Denis Chicola, Manager A/V Comm.
OptiLink	Maki Morris, Consultant
Patelco	Susan Gustavson, Marketing, Director
First Deposit Corp.	Walt Roder, SVP
Logo Paris	Diana Downs

The potential clients for whom we can deliver bottom-line related projects are:

Sola Optical	
Flora/Elkind Associates	Dan Flora, principal
Crouse and Associates	Bill Crouse, President
Pacific Stock Exchange	Betty Carter
Pringle & Associates	Joyce Pringle, principal
Symantec	Pam Fleming, Product Manager
	Maureen Dillon, VP Marketing
A T & E Corp.	Pamela Gamick, Corp. Comm. Asso.
Peterson & Dodge	Linda Peterson or David Skolnick

These potential clients have either contacted us or have been contacted by us sometime in 1988. They have either indicated a desire to produce videotapes or other types of communications or inquired as to our capabilities to do so. They constitute the base of potential clients which we will expand significantly in 1989.

The potential clients from whom we can generate fee-based income include:

Hewlett-Packard Co.	HPTV
Bank of America	Bob Ripley
	Dexter Loo
ByVideo	Jayleen Ryberg

Mervyn's	Mike Fleming
ComputerLand	Al Maggio
Pacific Bell	Susan Fetters
Time Arts	Laura Malone

Operational Objectives:

By February 28, 1989, we will implement a policy regarding our "Terms and Conditions" for doing work for clients.

We have been fortunate thus far to work for clients who pay their bills; however, we have experienced some slow-paying clients. We will therefore establish a more vigorous approach to receiving money earned within a specific time frame. To do that, we will implement a policy to receive up-front payment, and to ensure prompt payment of monies due at the completion of the project.

Some methods to ensure prompt payment include:

- Include the terms and conditions, as appropriate, in the proposal we submit to clients.

- Enforce the "net ten days" clause on our invoices by sending a follow-up invoice with interest added to the bill.

- Discuss the financial aspects of producing the project for the client when they commit to the job, or include a detailed paragraph in the proposal regarding payment of fees.

- This might include adapting the AICP contract's payment stipulations in the proposal or separate form with the client.

There are some equipment acquisitions we can make to enhance our stature with clients and potential clients, and to increase our overall productivity.

Currently, we spend relatively little for sending and receiving facsimiles of scripts or other data to and from clients. It is readily apparent, however, that "faxing" is on the increase.

At a store like CopyMat we might spend $15-$20 per document. With clients like Hewlett-Packard we are able to send and receive faxes without charge at the Rohnert Park plant. But whether we send or receive at H-P or at CopyMat, we have to leave the office. Generally, something is sent via fax because of the time-critical nature of the document. In other words, we're heavily involved in a project at the time. Leaving the office, more specifically, being away from the phone, can place a burden on our ability to manage the project underway.

At an average of $15 per document sent or received, we would fully pay back the purchase of a fax machine within one hundred document transmissions. That pay-back rate doesn't include the cost of driving to and from the facsimile machine's location.

By June 30, 1989, we will have completed the research, purchased and made operational a fax machine for $1,500 or less.

Another equipment acquisition that would enhance our productivity and could pay for itself over time is an off-line system

As it now stands, for fee-based projects we generally do the off-line editing at our client's facility, necessitating that we leave our office. Additionally, we must make our schedule fit that of our client's facility. For bottom-line projects, we off-line at Angel Productions, at an approximate out-of-pocket cost to us of $300 per project. Recent research shows us that to install a computer-based, time-code editing off-line system which would include monitors, cabling, IBM clone-computer, two tape decks and other pertinent material would run between $8,000 and $10,000. Therefore, payback for the system would occur about the 30th time we used the system. Given that we anticipate five bottom-line projects this year, payback wouldn't occur until the sixth year after purchasing the system, not taking into account the maintenance aspects of such a system. But it also doesn't take into account the money-savings gained from a more efficient on-line editing session, or the tax benefits from such an equipment purchase.

If we anticipate off-lining half of the fee-based shows with the system, however, payback occurs three years earlier. By doing that, we benefit in several ways.

First, we can accommodate our schedule, rather than the client's. In other words, we can complete the off-line at times that fit our needs, early morning or late in the evening. This will free us up to call on other clients, without being apparent to the client for whom we are off-lining.

Second, another advantage in having our own off-line system is that we enhance our value to our clients, because we can turn a project around faster than we could if the client's system(s) was being used by other people. It may also provide us an "air" of being a production company that so many first-time users seem to want.

Our experience using a computer-based off-line editing system on a 1987 project for the Federal Reserve Bank showed we can double our editing efficiency from about ten edits an hour to over twenty. Working on a bottom-line project, for example, could reduce an edit session from ten hours to five, giving us a cost-savings of $825. Such a savings reduces the payback period even more to under two years.

One other way to reduce the outlay of money to buy the system is to find a partner who could share the expense. Proximity with the partner would obviously be an issue, as would accessibility. Payback, however, might be even quicker.

By May 1, 1989, we will research feasibility of purchasing a computer-based off-line system, and given our findings and financial situation, we will purchase one and make it operational by October 31, 1989.

Factors in the decision . . .

- Compatibility with on-line editing systems at post-houses and client facilities.
- Flexibility of using our current computer system with the off-line system, thereby saving us the approximately $600 a clone may cost.
- Where would we put the system if we bought it?
- Is there a potential partner who might be interested in sharing the costs and benefits of such a system?
- How much maintenance is required, or customer support rendered by the system's seller?

- If we bought a portable computer on which we could load a computer-based off-line editing software program like EditLister, would that be more cost-effective and help us get "two birds with one stone?"

Earlier this year our computer went down, causing us a certain amount of anxiety. In periods of peak work or business development, this is a situation which we simply cannot afford. Also, when we're on the road visiting with several clients over the course of a day, our schedule is such that we might have significant breaks in between meetings. With a portable computer, we could work on proposals, or use the Tracker program to contact other clients.

By May 1, 1989, we will research and determine feasibility of purchasing a portable computer system which may utilize EditLister, interface with Angel Productions' editing system, and act as our back-up system within the office. Purchase will be based on financial status, but should be made by August 31, 1989, if such a purchase is feasible.

By January 31, 1989, we will compose and begin using a client checklist, a list of questions pertinent to discovering as much information about a client's project, budget, and the project's actual decision-makers.

By February 28, 1989, we will develop a five-year plan for growth to include projections about: facilities, personnel, products, services, market position, and financial situation.

CHAPTER 4

Managing Your Overhead and Other Money Issues

Your business plan can help you do more than give your business development a sharp focus. It can also help you do things like plan what kind of office equipment you need and anticipate where and how to find money to run the business or help you during lean times.

For example, computers continue to grow more powerful. Do you want to use a PC or a Mac or go both ways? Maybe you are already savvy on one system, and you don't want to change. Before I started on my own, I surveyed the businesses I planned to work with and found that virtually every one of them used PCs for daily business applications, so I chose to buy a PC. Since then, many businesses and many of my vendors began to use MacIntosh systems, so when I upgraded I chose a Power PC to be able to work with both PC or Mac software.

Voice mail, pagers, cellular phones and other communications devices are all easily affordable tools that can help you provide better service to your clients. Which tools do you need to use and how do you plan to integrate them? Your business plan will give you a good foundation to make those choices.

There are a couple of other important things to know and do to get your business off the ground.

Overhead and Your Office

As has been said often about money, it is the mother's milk of survival. Remember from Chapter 3 that one reason many businesses fail is because they are undercapitalized. You have to expect little or no income early on. If you have little or no overhead, you won't be strangled out of business.

If you can't handle money then you're going to have a tough time of it. Get a good accountant or bookkeeper to help you. My wife has been integral in the success of the business because I have used her as a sounding board when it came to business expenses, among other things. I also call my accountant regularly for advice and information. Though I only actually see him a couple of times a year, our relationship is a year-round one.

A Success Tip

If you don't use a lot of water in your garden, it's easier to adjust when you experience a drought.

When planning the business, I looked at the vendors who seemed to be the most successful to see how they operated their offices. Two role models in my own industry were very successful and worked out of offices in their homes.

I heard one national radio talk-show host say that you should never let on that you work out of your home. I listen to his radio program regularly, but I think he's out of touch with today's new work force. Every one of my clients knows I work out of my home, and I believe I never lost a job because of it.

Besides, with today's office technology there is virtually no reason to start a business selling your professional services by renting office space. If an office away from the home is truly important to you, get the business off the ground first, then shop around for the best rent you can get.

Exceptions to the Rules

A vendor of mine made a significant investment in technology to do what he needs to do. He also must meet routinely with clients. In his case, an office is an appropriate and professional thing to have.

Some people simply don't have the room at home. Maybe they have young children who are typically noisy throughout the day. Other people don't have the self-discipline to sit at a desk in their home and work. Some people just need to have a place to go.

Because only you know your strengths and weaknesses, you have to decide what is best for you. I strongly suggest that a major monthly expense can be eliminated by setting up an office in your home. Remember, less overhead gets you to profit sooner. If you really must have an office, consider subletting or renting from a business that has a little extra space. If the office already has a fax, copier and other office equipment, so much the better.

It used to be that an in-home office was an attractive tax-deduction. Recent IRS rulings have made it much less so. Ask your accountant to see if an in-home deduction is worth more than several hours of your accountant's time arguing with an IRS agent.

Technology in the Office

If you need certain technology immediately—like a computer, answering machine and fax—you should buy them. But maybe you don't need everything you think you need.

Consider the fax machine and the copier. Maybe you only need to have a fax card in your computer. I didn't buy a fax machine until I was in business for a couple of years. Why? I didn't send or receive faxes frequently enough to justify the expense. During that time, when I needed to send or receive a fax, a friend let me use his machine. Sometimes I paid him straight up—a per-page cost. Occasionally, I treated him to lunch for the favor. There are several businesses near me that offer fax service, too. On top of that, they also have a variety of copy machines and the ability to bind my proposals so that I can look as big league as any Fortune 500 company.

How big? A client told me long after our relationship was established that when I first called on her she thought she might not be able to afford me. My proposals and the way I presented them gave her the notion.

Credit Cards, Lines of Credit and Savings

Before going into business for yourself, and depending on whom you listen to, you should have anywhere from six months to a year of savings in the bank. On top of that, you should have no debt—except maybe a house payment. So if you have the luxury of planning to leave your company, pay down your consumer debt. All of it.

While you're at it, get as much credit as cheaply as you can before you leave your current job. Like farmers who borrow from the bank to buy seed in the spring only to pay the bank back after the harvest, credit used *wisely* can help you smooth out cash flow valleys. Until you have two years of established tax returns as a self-employed individual, you won't be able to get new credit. So get those credit lines established while you still have a regular paycheck coming in.

Why? Once you get rolling, credit can be a great ally. In 1995, I was working on several projects that had—at best—long-term pay-off potential. They were long sales cycles with no guarantees, but the potential return for each of the projects was significantly greater than what I was earning. The risks were worth our investment of time and money. We practically lived off of our credit lines for almost six months. But don't be fooled by my experience and go running out to take a flyer on something that carries a high risk. In August of that year, I produced *five* different projects to bring the credit lines back to zero. It was several weeks of 15-hour days and some fortuitous circumstances that allowed me to do that. I also lined up a couple of other programs that I could produce without a significant impact on the time I spent with the speculative projects.

My seven-year track record gave me the confidence to take the risks. Also, my wife and I had the discipline not to spend

---

Credit Can Help You Get Started

Ron and Kay Kramer own and operate All Computer Solutions, a company that designs and installs systems for businesses. They are also authorized dealers for companies like Apple, Hewlett-Packard and other companies.

Credit cards helped them launch their business.

"Ron and I had been frustrated entrepreneurs. We just wanted to take what we had done for years for somebody else and do it for ourselves," she said.

They used credit cards to finance their first year because they needed to establish their viability with suppliers.

"We took the first year in establishing our credibility and our terms with suppliers. It isn't an overnight thing. It's a long process. We're really able to handle the big projects now because we just slowly kept at it and did small projects until we had these enormous good terms and credit with our suppliers. We did it all at first with our personal credit. We didn't have any savings when we first opened up."

---

money needlessly, so our outgo wasn't too bad. We were also disciplined during periods of high income in the previous seven years to put money away. That ensured us that, if forced to, we could eliminate all of our debt and still have a nest egg.

Most professional service businesses usually don't carry inventory. If that describes your business and you are also a sole proprietor, there's another advantage to using credit wisely. As you complete projects at the end of the year, you can postpone billing for them until the next year. At the same time, you can use your credit (or your cash reserves) to accelerate the expenses you incurred on the projects. That means you can deduct the expenses in the current tax year but pay taxes on the income in the next tax year. Before you do anything, however, check with your tax adviser to ensure it's shrewd to do that.

The key word when using credit—however you use it—is *discipline*.

Establishing Credit for Your Business

The irony is that once you are in business for yourself, you will have to establish credit for your business. Suppliers and vendors will want some assurance that they'll be paid for the supplies or work they provide.

Until you have an established relationship with them, suppliers will usually expect you to pay immediately. Once that happens, however, you'll be surprised how quickly your suppliers are willing to grant you credit. If they aren't exposing themselves too much or if they were regular suppliers for you when you were on staff, they might be pretty easy with the credit early on.

Your current suppliers will likely be your resources when you go out on your own. So if you have an established relationship with them before you leave your staff position, it is very likely that they will extend credit to you immediately because they already know how you do business. The key is that you should be treating your vendors well while you are still working at International Industries or Acclimated Manufacturing.

Letterhead and Your Image

A project I was doing for a major bank brought me into one of the bank's branches. Just inside the staff room door was a full-length mirror. Above the mirror was a sign that said, "Your appearance is the first impression the customer has of the quality of service you deliver." It was obviously targeted at staff people who were just about to walk into the branch's public area, but it was—and still is—applicable to anyone working in a professional capacity. As the adage goes, "You never get a second chance to make a good first impression."

The first impression people will have of your quality of service often will be the opening letter you write. Regardless of your company's size, your letterhead and other presentation materials can make you appear to be as big as your largest competitor. I didn't believe that when I had my materials printed inexpensively in the beginning. After a while a good friend convinced me otherwise, and I spent the money to get materials designed and printed. Often, clients and prospects comment favorably on the quality of my business card, presentation materials and so on. I firmly believe now that investing in the design and printing of your stationery is worthwhile because it can be one early and important impression your prospects have of the quality of service you can deliver.

If you aren't a graphic designer, hire a good one to put together an identity package that includes letterhead, mailing labels and multipurpose cards that can be used for sending thank-yous or informal notes. If your business requires special packaging, make sure to use your design in that, too.

For example, I use videotape labels in my business, so I also printed labels that have my logo, address and phone number. The result? My clients often have my company logo sitting on their desks or bookshelves reminding them about my work even when I'm not around.

Managing Your Time Is a Money Issue

Death and taxes are certainties. If you are self-employed, another certainty is that you'll spend a lot more time doing things that other people did for you when you worked for International Industries. That means you will really need to manage your time. And if you plan to bill by the hour instead of the job, keeping accurate track of your time clearly has an effect on your bottom line. So now you have a different reason to watch that clock than when you worked for the corporation.

Even if 90 percent of genius really isn't showing up on time, *never* let your clients wait for you. Get a calendar system and use it. If you're going to be delayed getting to any meeting, by any means let the client know and give her the option to reschedule at her convenience.

How Much Should You Charge?

A survey of your friendly competitors or of vendors whose businesses are similar to yours will show you that it is possible to charge differently. For example, people I hire as directors of photography charge me anywhere from $375 per day to over $1,500 per day. They also have higher rates when we shoot film, as much as double what they charge for shooting video. Their basic rates differ for a few simple reasons.

Some are clearly better at what they do than others. Since the demand for their services is high and they only have so much supply (their time), they can charge more. Others, though their skills aren't quite as good, have the gumption to charge more anyway. They find enough people who will pay. There's another group who has the skills, but they don't have the confidence to ask what they should.

If you're going to be in the business of providing a professional service, you need to figure out how much you should charge. Do a survey. But don't stop there because the survey won't tell you how much money it costs to run your business or how much you need to live on. The following few steps will give you an idea of the minimum hourly or daily rate you need to charge for your services. If you are able to convince people to pay you more than that, so much the better.

First, determine how much money you want to make over the course of a year. You should include *all* of your expenses like taxes, retirement and so on. Now, add in the costs associated with your business. This includes phones, computers, car costs, insurance, other taxes, supplies and so on. The number you arrive at is the amount of money you must make to break even.

Next, figure out how many days you will work during the year. Not counting the weekends or national holidays, there are about 255 working days during the year. If you take two weeks off for vacation and include another week of sick days or days you probably won't work for a variety of personal reasons, you are down to 240 days. You also have to account for the days when you are working but not billing for your time—days you are upgrading computer software or developing business, for example.

Let's say you spend about 80 percent of your time doing work that is billable—192 days. If you want to bill by the hour, multiply 192 × 8 hours per day (or however many hours per day you expect to work) for your total hours worked. That gives you 1,536 hours. Then divide that into the amount of money you must earn to break even. If you want to bill by the day, divide 192 into the amount of money you must earn to break even. If you must earn $120,000 per year, and you plan to charge by the hour, then you must bill a little more than $78 per hour. If you plan to charge by the day, then you must bill $625 per day.

This simple formula does not account for the money you can make if you mark up the expenses you incur by hiring other vendors to do parts of your project. It does give you a sense of what you need to make to stay in business.

Charging enough is critical to staying in business as is establishing and maintaining a network of prospects, clients and others who can refer work to you, a process we'll look at in the next chapter.

CHAPTER 5

Establishing and Maintaining Your Network

Speaking of time management, avoid that deadly *analysis by paralysis*. You should analyze possibilities and potential outcomes but after a certain point just do it. You can make adjustments as you go.

Under the guise of trying to plan for the future, a vendor and friend who hasn't been in business all that long spends an inordinate amount of time trying to determine his customer base, estimate overhead costs, and to survey clients and potential clients about a variety of business issues. What the guy really needs to do is contact people, then go out and ask them for the business. Instead, he avoids it by trying to analyze the people who might buy his services. Unfortunately his offices are quieter than they should be—especially considering how much time he has spent analyzing his client base. Given all of his effort, it's understandable discouraging to him that business isn't rushing through his doors.

As with my early efforts to sell, he needs to make adjustments. Trust me, in the beginning, you'll have plenty of opportunities and time to tweak your own process. The best way to learn about your prospects is to get out there and meet them. You also will be making impressions—impressions that are critical to make to get business.

So, how do you meet the right people, the people who actually buy your services? Here are a couple of techniques I have used.

Start with Your Existing Network

Again, steal a little advice from novice insurance salespeople. Look to your existing network of friends, colleagues and vendors. For example, if you are still working at International Industries and you are responsible for working with printing companies, ask the people you buy from about other buyers like you. After all, if those other buyers do the same kind of work you do, they might be inclined to hire you when they have more work than they can handle.

Then Branch Out

Professional societies are also a great place to meet prospects. If you are currently in a professional society, go to the meetings and participate in the organization's activities. Arrive at events early and don't stand around with people you already know. Mingle. The best part about meeting people in such settings is that they are usually more receptive than they are at their offices during the business day.

Don't be concerned with selling. Do be concerned about making a positive impression. A positive impression generally comes from amiable, pleasant and interesting conversation.

"Gosh," you're saying, "I don't know what to talk about in situations like that. I always find the silence awkward." I did too, until I realized that the best way to have a conversation with someone I don't know is to ask them questions about *themselves*.

Establish Common Ground with Personal Questions

Ask general personal questions like, "How long have you been in your current job?" "How long have you been with your present company?" "What did you do before you took this job?" "Where did you go to school?"

Before long, you will likely find some common interest that will help you establish a personal relationship. It's important to be insatiably curious about the person, because you can't have a business relationship without first having developed some personal relationship. Be careful, though, to not dominate the person's time. After all, he's there to expand his network, too.

Once you've established personal contact, your next step is to ask for and get an appointment to meet with the prospect to discuss ways you can help him do his job. We'll talk more about the mechanics of that later.

Serendipity Builds Your Network, Too

Besides looking to your network of friends, colleagues and vendors or within professional societies, serendipity can be a good tool to help you establish your business. You simply have to be aware of opportunities, then take advantage of them when they arise. In my first year, two such occasions happened to me, and business that evolved from them still continues today.

In one situation, my wife and I went to dinner at a Japanese restaurant where eight people sit around the grill as the chef entertains the patrons with his deft knife work and patter. We were sitting with three other couples. Except for our individual dinner partners, none of us knew anyone else at the table. As dinner progressed, the group became more congenial. I began talking with a man who was general manager of a water district.

California struggles with dry summer months, so he wanted to show people in his water district what kind of landscape design worked best for our climate. He was just about to invest $20,000 in a demonstration garden at the water district's office. He hoped that people in the district would take the time to come by to see what a drought tolerant landscape looked like, and then install one around their houses.

I asked him if he had ever considered a videotape that could be distributed for free through nurseries or garden shops in his area. The cost for producing one could be about the same as a garden he installed at his office. The benefit was that people could check a tape out when they were actually in the process of enhancing their yards. He would be taking the demonstration garden to people who were interested.

Had I not met him—serendipitously—at dinner, I would have never considered him a prospect. He simply didn't fit my customer profile. I benefitted from serendipity because I was open to it.

Practice Insatiable Curiosity

I don't know if he would have been open to a sales presentation in his office. Some people have an aversion to sales people or to sitting through a sales presentation. But dinner in that restaurant was not an obvious sales situation. I didn't leave the house that night expecting to initiate a sale. I was insatiably curious. During our conversation he talked about the demonstration garden and about how he wasn't certain that he would be able to attract people to the garden.

By being curious about his situation, the light switched on for me. I didn't say to him, "You should have a video instead of an actual garden." I did ask, "If there was a way to bring the garden to the people, would you be interested?" He said, "Of course, but how?" Then I described my concept in a few brief sentences. He admitted he was intrigued, and we agreed to get together the following week in his office. Then I left it alone for the rest of the night, and enjoyed the evening. Ultimately, I was successful in making the sale, and he has been successfully using the program for almost a decade. On top of that, other water districts used it, and the program was also recut into several public service commercials for use in California.

Another time serendipity struck I was flying back from Toronto. I had just completed shooting a project for my first big client, a high-tech firm. During the flight I struck up a conversation with the gentleman next to me. I asked him what he did for a living. He turned out to be the third-party marketing manager for another high-tech company. Now *this* guy fit my client profile.

Again it was obviously not a sales situation. Still, my job for the next three hours was to build a personal relationship with him. It was easy to do that because I discovered we shared similar personal experiences. How? I asked a wide range of general, but personal, questions about his job, his department and about him.

My overall knowledge of his company helped me carry on the conversation. I had read a variety of periodicals and trade magazines and talked with others in my network. I knew long before I ever boarded that plane and sat next to him that his company used video extensively to communicate with employees and customers.

Deep into the conversation and well after a positive early relationship was established, I asked him about the company's video production capabilities. He gladly provided me with the names of two different women in his company who hired vendors like me.

As the plane taxied to the terminal, we exchanged business cards. I promised to let him know how things turned out. Of course, when I got into the office the next day I also sent him a personal note thanking him for the referrals.

I was hired by one of the women within weeks of that serendipitous meeting at 35,000 feet. She brought me in to create the company's new employee orientation videotape. Years later I still manage projects for the other woman.

Tracking Your Clients and Your Prospects

As you build your network, you will need some method of keeping track of people's phone numbers and addresses as well as notes you keep about your contacts with them. "What do you mean keep notes of my contact with them?" you may ask.

Remember, you are building personal relationships with people. During your conversations with a client or prospect, you'll hear about things like his unit's goals, his company's strategy, the ways he likes to conduct business, comments about people and other companies, what he likes to do in his spare time, what his expectations are of the people who work for him or for whom he works and more. After a while, if you continue to meet people, unless you have an archival memory, you won't possibly remember all of that critical information about everybody. You must keep notes.

A friend of mine uses a random-access, no-battery powered, standard number two pencil and note pad. Others I know use large Rolodex card files. When I started my business, I kept client notes in individual manila folders. Now I use a software program. For me, the beauty of that particular application is that I can access it when one of my clients calls. When I am going out for the day, I can also print out client phone numbers and notes to refer to when I call them.

I know that when my vendors call on me and can talk about things I am interested in, I am more likely to spend time talking with them. It pays to keep notes about things that are important or dear to your prospects and clients. You have to decide what method is best for you. Just figure out a technique that you like. It will pay dividends down the road.

A Board of Directors?

Another way to generate referrals is also a way you can gain access to valuable business advisers. Put together a board of directors. It can be formal or informal.

I am not suggesting that you should incorporate and bring in a group of people to sit around a table four times a year with you. What I am suggesting is that you turn to other people—experts in your field or in a field that is important to your success—for their wisdom and experience.

I learned about the concept of a board of directors as advisers from a woman whose business was managing major events for companies. She organized an experienced group of people to advise her about building her business. She brought together a cross section of advisers whose participation would also be a valuable networking tool for themselves. Among them were a couple of people who "anchored" the board. Like shopping centers that have large anchor tenants to attract shoppers, she had a couple of mentors whose presence helped her fill the other seats. These advisers helped her grow a very successful business that she eventually sold to a group of her employees for a couple of million dollars.

I have an informal board. They have never met, but I often talk with them individually, seeking their advice about the many choices I can make as my business evolves. Only a couple of them actually are aware that I look to them as advisers.

Likely Board Members

Who should be on the board? It should consist of people who you need to tap for whatever advice you need to run your business, expand it or take it in a different direction. Each of them should bring a different discipline or perspective and some knowledge about you and your industry.

As I said earlier, my board is an informal one that never meets. I consider these people part of my board because I often turn to them for critical advice to run my business effectively. My banker, my accountant, my insurance broker and my lawyer all serve in obvious professional advisory capacities. So they are on my board.

A friend with a strong general business background whom I have known since college is also an adviser. He knows nearly every financial detail of my business because we talk two or more times a week, and he provided his input about my business as I grew it.

I also turn for advice to another friend who is a banker and who was a client when I worked for a paycheck. He provides a dispassionate perspective from 400 miles away.

Also on my board is a role model who has been in the same business much longer than I have and a mentor who hired me out of college and has watched me make just about all of the mistakes possible in the world. They provide significant input when I call.

Finally, my wife was chief operating officer of a $120 million credit union. She managed 45 people, and she dealt with a myriad of vendors on a daily basis. She obviously knows me, and she has a strong understanding of what it takes for me to succeed.

As I said, my board is not a formal one. I chose that style because it suited me better. They can be candid when I seek business advice because they know me personally.

Having a more structured board makes things more complicated but can also provide even more benefits in terms of referrals and so on. Remember that board members should be of sufficient reputation that it makes their referrals very helpful when you develop business.

Regardless of the Advice, It's Still Your Decision

How beneficial can a board—informal or otherwise—be for you? In one case my role model gave me some tips on cutting my insurance costs by almost two-thirds. Another experience had nothing to do with getting business as much as it did with staying in business.

Early on, I had an opportunity to take a job with a financial services industry giant. Besides no longer being self-employed, it would have meant that we relocate to Manhattan. The offer was enticing. My wife and I talked about it. She was willing to move if the job was really something I was interested in. I was interested; I just wasn't certain if it was a move I should make.

So I called a couple of my advisers. Now, obviously, my lawyer, accountant and banker wouldn't be that helpful. But I talked to my two friends who knew me very well and to my role model who would know whether such a job would provide that much of a career boost.

It would, in fact, be a career boost, said my role model. He also said the offer deserved long consideration. I already agreed with him.

But it was the conversations with both of my friends that enlightened me and helped me decide not to go. One suggested that he thought I really wanted to be self-employed and that I hadn't given self-employment much of a shot.

He was right. I did prefer being my own boss. It was what my wife and I planned for, and I had not given the business enough time to get off of the ground.

Though I turned to other people to discuss the opportunity, in the end it was still my decision. That's the part I like best about being self-employed. Ultimately, you make the decisions necessary to run, grow or change the direction of your business. And, of course, you are also responsible to sell what you do. To do that effectively, sooner or later you have to find the real buyer, not somebody who looks like one.

CHAPTER 6

Finding the Real Buyer

Often, one reason why people don't like to sell is because they perceive people who sell to be like Herb Tarlick on *WKRP in Cincinnati*. So don't be like Herb Tarlick. The best way to sell professional services is to develop a personal relationship with your prospects and clients. To do that, be yourself.

How? Identify what you like and what you don't like when someone is selling to you. This will give you an understanding of your own sales personality. Maybe you like a soft sell. Perhaps you like to interact with someone who helps to drive you to a buying decision, a harder sales approach.

┌──┐
│ **Telephone Tip** │
│ │
│ When you call, always ask if the prospect has the │
│ time to talk. │
└──┘

If you have already established a good relationship with a couple of clients, ask them how you convinced them to hire you. Formally or otherwise, try to speak with other buyers of your services to determine how they like to be approached.

For example, I am always amazed when somebody interrupts my day by cold calling me on the phone and begins jabbering away before I even have the chance to tell them that I don't buy what they are selling or that I am busy. If the person simply asked me if I had a moment to spare, I'd be more inclined to speak with him briefly then or longer at a later time.

Of course, when selling you still have to be able to read and react to many personalities that are unlike yours. To truly thrive, continue to ask yourself, "What makes this person tick?"

Regardless of your sales personality, one of the challenges to being successfully self-employed is finding the actual buyers of your services within the corporate bowels of International Industries' competitors. How do you do that?

Some People Can't Say "No," But They *Do* "No"

It's an important issue, because you can waste a lot of time and energy calling on someone who isn't really the buyer.

I attended a national conference for a professional organization to which I belonged. A senior executive I used to work for happened to be on a panel with another senior executive from another financial institution. After the presentation, I went up to say hello. My former boss turned to his peer and said, "This fellow did a lot of great video work for me. You should use his skills." What a gracious referral!! She told me to call her the following week, which I did enthusiastically.

She referred me to the manager of the bank's video production group. Of course, I did as the executive recommended and called the manager to arrange an appointment.

When I arrived for the meeting, the manager's secretary seemed surprised to see me. Evidently, her manager had planned for over a month to take that day off. An apparently innocent mistake had been made, so I called back the following day to arrange another appointment.

When I arrived for the make-up meeting the secretary stammered as she explained that the manager I was to see was in an all-day staff meeting—one that had been planned for some time.

I put on my best face, smiled and told her I would call the following day for another appointment.

The third time I showed up, I was certain I would see the video manager. She had made and broken two appointments with me. Plus the executive she reported to had told her to see me. Surely she would at least follow those instructions. Wrong.

For the third straight time the video manager stood me up. This time the secretary told me that the manager's friend had unexpectedly passed away and that she was attending the funeral. Sure, I thought callously, and my dog ate the homework.

Obviously, that wasn't a very sensitive perspective on my part, especially if the woman's friend really had passed away. Still, since my meeting had been scheduled for the afternoon, the courtesy of a phone call from the secretary to keep me from coming in would have been nice.

Since whining never presents a good image, I put on my best face again, told the secretary how sorry I was to hear about her boss's friend, and that I would call the following day to arrange another appointment. With half a smile, I also suggested that all of these missed appointments would be to my benefit. Having stood me up three times, her boss must feel a little guilty. I expected that she would give me her full attention when we did finally meet.

So Don't Take "No" Personally

On my fourth try, the manager was there to see me. She extended a friendly greeting and escorted me to her office.

I like to explore the prospect's needs and discuss how the prospect works with vendors, then show my demo reel. She threw me a curve by grabbing and promptly playing my demo reel. About two minutes into my ten-minute demo, she just stood up and walked out of the room. No explanation. No information about how long she would be gone. She just left.

I stopped the tape, backed it up and waited for her to return. When she did I started the tape again. A couple of minutes later she was beating feet again. Same thing—no explanation, just an exit stage right. So I stopped the tape and waited for her to come back.

She returned nearly ten minutes later with no explanation or apology, so I started the tape again. Darned if she didn't leave a third time.

After she reappeared to sit through the final couple of minutes, she asked what I charged for my work. I told her. We ended the meeting on a cordial note. She instructed me to call a fellow who reported to her, the department's production manager. He was on vacation, but she said to contact him when he returned.

I did that, but before I ever talked with him, my evasive prospect's secretary intercepted my call. The secretary was instructed to tell me that I cost too much. In effect, "Thanks for your interest, but don't let the door hit you on your you-know-what."

When I tell the story to my colleagues and vendors, they usually react by saying how rude the woman was. It would certainly have been nicer if she'd have told me she wasn't interested and it would have saved us both a lot of time. Unfortunately some people just can't do that, and you better not take their inability to say "no" personally.

The scenario unfolded badly because of two reasons. The prospect avoided seeing me, but didn't have the gumption to tell me she didn't want to meet. When we finally did get together, I didn't control the situation. I wasn't necessarily intimidated, but by being painfully polite I let her waste our time. The biggest problem was that I dealt with the wrong person. When the secretary told me that my rates were too high, she also told me that even though her boss was the department manager, the production manager was the real buyer.

The moral of the story? The division head, the department head or some other titular being is not necessarily the buyer.

Real Buyers Are in a Variety of Places

You can find buyers in a variety of places. As I described earlier, serendipity is one place. Don't plan on building a client list using serendipity, though. The best places to look are professional organizations, personal referrals by other professionals or friends, professional trade periodicals and local business news. Let's talk about each one.

Professional Organizations in Your Industry

Professional organizations that cater to people in your profession are a good place to find buyers. Remember, one of the purposes of these groups is to have meetings where ideas and knowledge are exchanged and to provide a vehicle for networking. People are more open to being approached at these meetings.

Also, these groups usually have lots of committee work that needs to be done. Volunteer to help because you'll work side by side with others who might just buy your services or who might be able to recommend you to someone who does. In these situations, you'll be building personal relationships that will be the foundation for your business's success. If you are still employed, your company may pick up your expenses for annual dues or trips to the national convention because your employer will benefit by your participation.

If you are still with International Industries and planning to go out on your own, join one or two of these professional groups before leaving and participate in their activities. Because you are still on staff, you'll be seen as a *buyer* of services. This perception will allow you to more easily establish personal relationships with other buyers, helping you to sow the seeds of a network long before you ever need to harvest it for work later when you are self-employed. So, if you have the luxury of planning to start your own business rather than think of a company name at the Surf-N-Suds, get involved in professional organizations now to begin building your client base. There is nothing deceptive about that. It's just planning ahead.

If you've already left the Surf-N-Suds wondering where you can get business cards printed, professional organizations are still an important place to look for buyers of your services. Go to the meetings. Get involved in the activities. Do great volunteer work. Get noticed. Especially in the early stages of your business, professional organizations are a good way to be productive while you're trying to get busy.

Professional Organizations in Other Industries

Another place to find buyers is in professional organizations of other industries. Let's say you are a copywriter and you do a lot of work in the financial services industry. Consider participating in the Financial Institutions Marketing Association. Since it includes people who need copywriters with your experience, you have a good chance of meeting people who will hire you.

If you are a graphic designer and work in Northern California, the wine industry does a lot of print work. Join a group that includes wine marketers to get into the loop creating graphics for them.

Nonprofit Organizations

Nonprofit organizations always need people with professional skills. Often these organizations have a board of directors made up of influential people. Helping nonprofits does two things. First, it is doing good work for people who need it. Second, it gives you good exposure to people who may have the capacity to hire you.

Every year I try to do at least one pro bono project as a way to give back to my community. It's an opportunity to meet and work with some really terrific people, too, extending my network as I go.

Choose the Organizations Carefully

Professional organizations cost money. If International Industries will pick up the tab for your membership and trips to the national conferences, all the better. Also, attending meetings and otherwise being involved in trade groups and nonprofit groups take a lot of time, so pick and choose your organizations carefully. Ask to see a membership list before you commit. Are the members people who can hire you?

When I first started my business, I joined a chamber of commerce thinking that I would meet a lot of buyers there. I was wrong. Not only did it cost me a couple of hundred dollars to sign up, I spent a lot of time doing volunteer work hoping to meet people who might buy my services. Unfortunately, the people who participated in that particular chamber weren't buyers of my services. It wasn't the chamber's fault, but I blew the investment because I didn't consider the businesses that made up the chamber.

I recommend being involved in one organization related to your professional industry, one or maybe two that cater to your potential buyers, and one nonprofit that can really use your skills. Remember to select them carefully.

Periodicals, Journals and Newspapers

Professional and trade periodicals, business journals and business sections of the daily paper are also places to look for buyers. Of course, you don't have the opportunity to establish a personal relationship before you contact them. Plus you are going to have to compete for their attention with lots of others like you who look for prospects in the same place.

Still, these can be useful places to troll. Why? Because such articles help you to know more about the prospects—even qualify them. Sometimes an article will tell you something personal. Other times it might describe a need that you can fill.

Government—Federal, State and Local

Many professionals find business with federal, state and local government buyers. Personally, I find the process of bidding on government projects to be more work than it is worth to me. Just getting qualified as a small business supplier with the State of California took me over two years, for example.

Still, many people have great success doing it. Laws require that government entities publicly announce requests for pro-

---

Look for Personal Information

Gretchen Hirsch, president of Stevens/St. John Company, provides writing, editing and communications management for companies. She gets information about people from mutual friends and colleagues, as well as from newspapers.

She was about to call on the president of a company that makes store fixtures: "There was an article in the paper. The company president whom I'd known for years but only tangentially, had a coronary, and I did not know that until I saw it in the paper. So when I went in to see him, I was able to sit down and ask, 'How are you doing?' And that starts a whole new ball game because I'm not just interested in coming in and taking the business. I want to know how he and his family are doing."

---

posals. Your local library carries publications that list these announcements. Those publications will also tell you what it takes to qualify to bid. You can even subscribe to publications that announce requests for proposals.

As with finding business contacts in periodicals, a lot of your competitors look for business in government publications. So the bidding is fierce, profit margins are smaller as a result and the odds of winning the business are slimmer than when you find clients on your own.

Referrals

Referrals from your friends, colleagues and suppliers are generally the best way to get business. When someone refers you to business or helps you out in any other way, common courtesy says to send the person a thank-you note. Astoundingly, common courtesy isn't so common.

In one situation, I referred someone to a client of mine. It was a $10,000 project that ultimately led to additional work for the woman I referred. I not only never got a word of thanks from her, I had to call to find out how the project went. Because it was my client, I had a vested interest in the referral. It took me four calls to find out!

My network of colleagues is a great asset, and I love sharing it with my clients because it makes me more valuable to them. When I refer someone, I want to know that it went well; and if it didn't, I want to know what happened. Conversely, if someone refers me to a client, I make certain to call immediately to thank them for the referral, and I promise to let them know how the project works out. If I get the business, I make certain to send the person who referred me a basket of wine, cheeses and fruit along with a thank-you card. At the very least, I send a handwritten note of thanks.

A Gesture of Thanks Goes a Long Way

People are sometimes floored when they receive my small gesture of gratitude—usually because no one has ever thanked them before. As a result, my genuine act goes a long way to create good will. Also, thanking people for their help is a courteous gesture that all of us should practice.

CHAPTER 7

Creating Your Presence with the Introductory Letter and First Phone Call

As you develop your list of prospects, start contacting them. Do not wait until your list is perfect. Remember, you will have plenty of time to make adjustments; so get to work.

If you haven't already met the prospect socially or at a professional meeting, your first contact will be by letter. Not just any letter, but an introductory letter that is four brief, single-spaced paragraphs on one page. The objective of the introductory letter is to get the prospect to take your call so that you can ask for an appointment.

The Elements of a Four-Paragraph Letter

In the first paragraph, describe how you got the prospect's name. In the second paragraph, state what you can do for the prospect. In the third paragraph, outline how you have helped similar companies in similar ways. In the fourth paragraph, tell the prospect when to expect your call.

The last paragraph is also a contract with yourself to call the prospect. After all, if you can't follow through on a commitment to call, then how can you sell yourself as a professional committed to meeting the person's deadline or budget? The letter should give the prospect enough information about you so that he or she will take your call.

It should go without saying that the letter should be cleanly printed. Some laser printers are cheap now. Given the professional look and graphics capabilities that laser printers offer, you should buy one. At the very least, the letter should be typewritten and without typos or misspellings. It should also be on quality paper with at least your name and address printed on it. The letter should be sent in an envelope that matches your letterhead.

An example of a good business letter appears on page 76. Straight and to the point, this type of letter doesn't beat around the bush and serves as a letter of introduction in an efficient way.

On the other hand, there is the letter which costs you time to write and money to send but is very unlikely to get the prospect to take your call, let alone schedule an appointment with you.

A lousy letter appears on 77. The only good thing about this letter is that it is one page long. If you are going to take the trouble to send a letter, find out exactly who your contact is before you write the letter. That way, you will know it is routed to the right person. And make sure you have the recipient's name spelled correctly and have her correct title. If you are not sure, call the company's main number or the prospect's secretary to ask for the correct spelling and proper title.

If you have experience *tell* the prospect. Don't be shy or modest. You want the work. To get it you need to tell the person how successful your similar projects were for other companies. The letter should include enough information about you to make the prospect want to speak with you. And only send a resumé when you are applying for a staff job or if the prospect asks you to do so.

Don't ask to have the prospect call you at his or her earliest convenience. And don't suggest that the prospect call you. You have to have enough gumption to make the call. For one thing, it shows the prospect that you have a proactive approach to doing business.

A LETTER WORTH SENDING

July 24, 1998

It's addressed to a specific person.

Jenna Nicholas
Vice-President—Sales
International Industries
10589 Casa de Pulgas Avenue
San Mateo, CA

Here's how you got her name.

Dear Jenna,

Here's how you can help the prospect.

A mutual friend and colleague, Donna Cavalin, suggested I contact you. Because our firm played a critical role in designing and executing her firm's most recent product announcement, she thought we might play a similar role in the upcoming roll out of your newest processor.

Our extensive experience with the business press, along with over 60 teleconferences under our belt, illustrates that we have the capabilities you need. On top of that, we are able to deliver these services for up to 15 percent less than the current industry average.

Don't be shy about your experience!

Besides helping Donna's firm on several similar projects, Brennan & Associates has also designed and executed the communications surrounding six other product announcements in the past two years. As a direct result of our efforts, companies like Widget Worldwide, Countryside Components, Myriad Matrix and others achieved greater press coverage than they expected.

You're committing to yourself as much as the client. Mark it in your calendar and do it!

I would like to discuss ways we can do that for you. Please expect my call on Wednesday, August 30th, to arrange a meeting with you to do just that.

Sincerely,

Gregory F. Brennan

A LETTER NOT WORTH THE BOTHER

July 24, 1998

*What
is it
that
you
want
to do?
What
is it
that
you
can
do?
What
kind of
experi-
ence
are
you
offer-
ing?*

Vice-President—Sales
International Industries
10589 Casa de Pulgas Avenue
San Mateo, CA

*This will be sent directly
to the round file with
the rest of the junk mail.*

To whom it may concern,

I am interested in working with your company. I am
prepared to make a commitment in a position that will
capitalize on my significant experience. I have worked
for a variety of companies and am currently looking for
more opportunities.

I have enclosed a resume and copies of two letters of
reference. I look forward to hearing from you soon
regarding an interview.

Sincerely

Gregory F. Brennan

*Only send a resume if
you are looking for a
staff job. Also, you
call them. . .*

A Four-Paragraph Letter for the Newly Self-Employed

If you have only recently left International Industries or
Acclimated Manufacturing and haven't had many—or any—
opportunities on your own, you can still use a four-paragraph
introductory letter with some minor modifications.

Again, the first paragraph opens by telling the prospect how
you got her name. The first paragraph also describes how your
skills might be applicable to the prospect's situation, project or
both. The second paragraph gives more specific details about
the project or projects that you believe are applicable to the
prospect's situation. The third paragraph uses a broad brush to
paint a picture of other skills and capabilities you have to offer

the prospect. The fourth, of course, is that all-important contract with yourself to call the prospect.

A letter for the newly self-employed appears on page 79.

Calling for the Appointment

After you send the letter, your next step is to call the prospect to arrange an appointment. There is a hidden benefit in using the telephone when talking with your prospect the first time. You can use a script. The script will provide helpful support if you are nervous. Using a script can also help you prime the conversation pump. Especially early in your business, rehearse your call before you actually make it. Of course, you don't want it to *sound* scripted or like you are a telemarketer either.

> ### Four Questions for Your First Phone Call
>
> • How big is your department, division or unit?
> • How often do you go outside for support?
> • What forces within the company cause you to go outside (or not)?
> • What vendors do you currently use to meet your additional needs?

Also, before you call, generate a list of questions to ask the prospect. The purpose of the questions is to pour the foundation of a good relationship.

Busy people will be more likely to need your help, so those are the people you should be calling. Since they're busy, you don't want to use up a lot of their time. That means you don't need to ask all of the questions you have prepared.

Ask the ones which the direction of the conversation allows you to ask. Those questions can be about the prospect's personal goals, about his organization's goals and objectives, things that would help or prevent him from meeting those goals and

ANOTHER LETTER WORTH SENDING

It's sent to a specific person—as with the first letter.

July 25, 1998

Connor Vincent
Vice-President—Sales
Global Structures
180 Montgomery Blvd.
San Francisco, CA

Tell the prospect how you got his name or remind him how you met.

Dear Connor,

It was a pleasure meeting you at last week's Motivational Sales regional conference. During our conversation, you mentioned that your firm needs a corporate sales training program, but your company's lean staffing requirements are inhibiting the program's development. Because I created and launched such a program when I was with Widget Manufacturing, I have the expertise to help you get your program launched.

Remind him of his situation and tell him how you can help him.

You also mentioned that your firm requires a strong multinational element for the program to succeed. Widget Manufacturing did, too. In that project I used today's communications technology to coordinate program development in Asia and Europe—but I never left the United States. Best of all, the president of Widget Manufacturing attributed the 15 percent increase in sales over six months directly to the program's implementation.

Don't be modest about your experience— especially your results!

Offer him other skills, too!

Besides that successful corporate sales training program, I developed motivational programs, promotional events for our largest customers and much more. As I said, I believe I can provide the expertise you need to bring your project to fruition.

I would like to discuss my ten years of experience at Widget Manufacturing and the ways your firm can take advantage of my skills. Please expect my call on Wednesday, August 30th, to arrange a meeting with you to do just that.

Sincerely,

Gregory F. Brennan

Don't forget your contract with yourself to call.

operational issues about his group and the way it meets the company's business objectives.

As with your letter, your call should be brief and to the point. If you start to get cold feet when you dial, don't balk now because you will probably only get the voice-mail recording of your prospect. This is particularly true with very busy people. Again, you are pouring the foundation for the relationship with this call, but the only objective is to get an appointment to see him.

It's All in How You Ask—Telephone Etiquette

Start your call with, "Hello, Jenna. This is Greg Brennan from Brennan Communications. I sent you a letter last week about our capabilities for helping companies with new product announcements. I wonder if you had a chance to read it and if this is a good time for you to talk?"

Then, stop talking and start listening. She might say that she saw your letter but hasn't had a chance to read it. In that case, ask again if it is a good time for her to talk. You want her full attention for just a few minutes. If she can't spare it, offer to call her back. If she says she can talk, simply reiterate your letter, stating who referred you and why, how you helped others in a similar situation and how you might be able to help her.

Some people don't like to take unplanned calls. That's okay. Let the prospect know a specific time when you are available—or even set an actual appointment to talk by telephone.

If She Doesn't Have the Time

She might say this isn't a good time to talk. In that case say, "Then I'm sorry for having interrupted you. Is tomorrow or Friday a good day to call back?" After she decides which day, then ask, "Is morning or afternoon better." When she chooses one, set a specific time, "Is 9:30 a good time to reach you? Or is 11:00?" Again, you've given her a choice, but if she wants to, let her pick another time. Then thank her for her time, tell her you look forward to speaking with her and conclude the conversation.

If She Does Have the Time

She might say she has just a moment to spare. In which case, say, "As I said, I sent you a letter describing ways my company helped Donna Cavalin, a colleague and mutual friend, to do similar work regarding product announcements. She thought I might be able to provide the same support for you." Briefly reiterate your letter, then pause to hear what the prospect has to say. She might want to talk about how you met Donna, the mutual friend. Briefly explain, then ask how she met Donna. She might describe how she was impressed by a certain project in which you may have had a hand. If so, tell her what your role was in that project and ask her about her most recent project (you should have gotten some background information from Donna about Jenna before you called her). She might tell you that she doesn't usually use outside resources. Ask her why that is.

It Should Be an Easy Back and Forth

The opening conversation is like a warm-up for a tennis match in that you lob a serve (a question) so the prospect can make an easy return with an informative answer. Through such a process you will glean more information from her, getting her to open up along the way. It should *not* be like the middle of a championship match where you keep firing questions at her.

At a point in the conversation that seems comfortable to you, ask to meet with her to show her a sample or samples of your work and to talk further about ways you might be able to help her meet some or all of her goals. "The meeting will only take about a half hour of your time," you should promise.

As I said earlier, you are going to get more work from people who are really busy. You want to make certain that you do not waste their time—or yours—by having a meeting to present your skills and expertise drag on.

Notice that I have assumed familiarity with the prospect in the introductory letter and on the phone by using her first name. I have a friend who feels more comfortable being more formal with prospects, addressing them as Mister, Miz, and so on until they ask to be called by their first name. I believe it is best to assume the familiar instead because you are trying to build a personal relationship, though there are times when position or seniority demands that you take a more formal stance. Your personality and style should dictate your approach.

Also, when you talk with a prospect, ask questions that elicit a positive response. Rather than ask, "How about calling you on Monday?" which would allow her only a "Yes" or "No" response, ask by offering an alternative. "May I call you on Monday or Tuesday? Morning or afternoon? Early or late?" According to age-old sales advice, asking questions that give your prospect a choice prevents the prospect from saying "No" to you. It is a twist of what those in sales circles call the "Alternative of Choice" close. In this case, you are selling the prospect—closing the prospect—on giving you an appointment.

What If the Prospect Won't See You?

Very frequently people will not schedule an appointment with you because they don't have the time or a reason to buy your services. You are not being rejected. Be polite and ask to call back periodically. How often? Call frequently enough that the prospect remembers you, but not so often that you get to be a pain in the behind. But you must call back regularly, because if you don't get the appointment, you will not get the business.

"I don't want to irritate a prospect and lose the opportunity to get her business," you say. Fine, but if you don't continue to ask for an appointment, you'll never get one. If you don't get the appointment, you won't get the business.

What If the Prospect Blows You Off?

There are times when you can follow all of these steps and the prospect simply puts you off or when you can tell from the tone in her voice that you are a bother. Certainly it will do neither of you any good if you try to press for anything during that phone call. At the very best, the prospect will just not be receptive. Worst case—she very likely might resent you enough to *never* take a call from you again.

Your call might go something like this:

"I sent you a letter last week that described my background. I was wondering if you had a chance to read it, and if you might be able to spare a few moments to talk?"

"There's never a good time to talk," she might hiss. Or she might not reply favorably to any of your open-ended questions. She might say, "Try calling me next month."

So, what do you do? The best thing is to politely end the conversation. But try very hard to leave the door open to call her at another time that may be more convenient for her—even next month as she may have suggested. After all, she may simply be having one horrible day, week or month. You are at a disadvantage because you have no idea whether she is or not.

Say, "I'm sorry I got you when you are so busy. I'll be glad to call back in a week (or whenever she suggests)." Then mark it down in your calendar to get back, and be sure to follow up. Again, pleasant persistent calling may open the door for you. If it doesn't, you probably never would have gotten business from her anyway.

You can't take the prospect's bad day or hectic schedule personally. You called at the wrong time. Not everyone has a good day every day, though normal people don't wake up in the morning planning to be curmudgeons.

I reiterate that the people who are busiest are the best clients, because once they trust your ability to take items off of their "To Do" list, they are going to call you. In other words, once your client trusts you to do what he would do in similar situations, you're virtually guaranteed to hear from him very frequently.

On the other hand, some people just do not have good interpersonal skills and may be off-putting when you call. It has only happened to me a couple of times, but I must admit it caught me off-guard when it happened.

Once I contacted a woman who managed the video communications group of a stock brokerage firm. Because I had done a project for the company before she got there, and because I had done some other projects related to stock, money and commodities trading, it was natural for me to call on her company.

I sent my four-paragraph introductory letter and followed with a phone call. She was not in, but I left her a voice-mail message. I called back a couple of days later. Same thing. On my third phone call, she answered.

When I asked her if she had a moment to talk she abruptly said, "We are not a good match. We can't work together. I use other companies that I am very happy with." I stumbled briefly because, other than my letter, she had no other information that I knew about on which she could base such a statement. She had not yet seen my demo reel, nor had we discussed my fairly significant experience that I believed she would find useful.

So I said, "I certainly appreciate that you might feel that way—and saying so will save you and me the time and effort of meeting. But, since I have you on the phone and so that I understand better the kinds of companies you are working with, may I ask what other vendors you do use?" Knowing who she was already using would give me at least a clue about why she so abruptly told me why we would not work together.

Then she floored me. "That's none of your business," she said.

While it may not have been my business, no one had ever said it to me before. In fact, only one other prospect ever refused to disclose the vendors he used. He simply said that it was confidential information and that he was sorry he could not say more.

Since I couldn't really think of anything else to say to the stock brokerage prospect, I thanked her for her time and laid the handset in the phone's cradle. Then I stared at the telephone for quite some time as I replayed the conversation over and over in my head—never really finding an answer for the way she acted.

Ultimately, I realized that all of us are different. It has been said, "It's not that it *takes* all kinds, it's because there *are* all kinds." People are going to treat you in a way you might not expect or want. Still, don't let the threat of being treated rudely get in the way of calling on people. It just doesn't happen often enough to be a problem or concern.

Odds Are You'll Only Get the Prospect's Voice Mail

It's much more likely that you write your telephone script, pen perfect questions, get all fired up and call your prospect, only to get her voice mail. What do you do then? Simple. Leave a message. However, it is equally important that you have your script rehearsed, because you don't want to record a message that makes you sound like a moron either.

A lot of voice-mail systems allow you to play your message back and rerecord it if necessary. Such a system usually tells you to press a specific number from your touch-tone phone for special sending options. Still, since you won't know until it's too late, have your initial script rehearsed to sound smooth and competent on your first personal contact.

As you would have if you talked directly to the prospect, restate the purpose of your call. If someone referred you, make certain that you say who it was and why. Then tell her that you'll call back at a specific time. Again, it is as much a contract with yourself as it is a courtesy to your prospect. Also, it shows that you are truly interested in talking with the prospect.

A former boss never talked with a pursuing vendor unless the person called five times. My boss believed that five calls proved the vendor was truly interested in selling my boss something.

Often, the prospect's voice mail will tell you when he'll return to the office. If the prospect is going to be out of the office for more than a couple of days, allow a day or two after he returns to contact him. Why? Odds are high that he'll be dealing with a lot of operational issues and other corporate stuff that arose while he was out. He'll be more likely to talk with you when he isn't so pressed with backed up business.

Also give the prospect the opportunity to call back at his convenience. Provide him with a time that you know he can reach you. Obviously, leave your number, leave it *slowly* and repeat it.

It Takes Perseverance To Succeed!

One study showed that 80 percent of all new sales are made after the fifth call on the same prospect. Nearly half of the people who call on new business call once, then never call again. About a third of all sales people make a second call, then stop. A few more stop calling after the fourth try on the prospect. Only one in ten people call enough times to turn a prospect into a new client.

Remember that prospects are just like the rest of us. Some will be willing to meet with new people after only a couple of contacts—or even one. Some people may take more effort to see. Some, not wanting to waste their time or yours, simply will not meet with you until there is something to talk about—that is, a tangible project on which your services might come in handy. Regardless, you need to get an appointment because it is nearly impossible to get business—especially professional services business—unless you have established a relationship with the prospect.

But let's be positive about this. If you have properly targeted your prospect and presented your case and capabilities, you will probably get the appointment. Think back to when you worked for International Industries. When you were hiring vendors, you probably felt like you never could have too much good talent waiting to meet the company's needs. Most smart people on staff feel that way. In fact, since International Industries and others down the street have reorganized, they don't have anyone on staff anymore who can quite do what you do, so they *need* to talk with you.

Telephone Tip

Whenever you leave your phone number, leave it *slowly,* and repeat your number.

Now let's talk about your appointment.

CHAPTER 8

Succeeding at the Appointment

Before you go, set some objectives. There should be at least three things you come away with from your first meeting with a prospect. You should find out what the prospect needs. You should find out what the prospect wants. You should also find out what the prospect will pay. Discovering these three things is necessary to make any professional services business succeed.

Back in 1992 when Ross Perot was running for president, he needed advertising. Since he has some pretty deep pockets, one could easily assume that he could afford the very best. In fact, Perot called Hal Riney, the creative genius behind a lot of America's great advertising in the '80s and an advertising force in Ronald Reagan's successful presidential campaigns.

Legend has it that Riney told Perot it would cost about $100,000 to produce a television commercial. Perot sniffed that he could get one produced in Dallas for $5,000. Both men were right. Regardless, Riney never created a commercial for Perot's campaign.

As with anyone who sells professional services, Riney needed to determine what Perot wanted, what Perot needed and what Perot would pay. With two successful presidential campaigns behind him, Riney knew what Perot needed. Perot, one of

America's richest men, could easily afford the expense of a first-rate advertising campaign. Figuring out what Perot *wanted to pay* was Riney's challenge.

Each man may disagree on how and why things broke down. What both can agree to is that Perot never had the chance to benefit from Riney's magic touch.

The Reverse Interview

So, selling professional services—regardless of scale—boils down to discovering what the prospect wants, needs and will pay. How do you do that? Ask questions.

A stock brokerage firm ran a series of ads about the firm's ability to successfully plan for their clients' future financial needs. The key message in the spots was brought home with someone asking, "How did they know you would need that?" and the firm's client responding, "They asked."

Be Helpfully Nosy

Regardless of the importance of asking prospects and clients about business goals and personal goals, about operational issues and personal issues, about financial objectives and so on, there are some people who say, "I can't ask those questions. That's being too nosy." Hogwash. It's the only way you can get the customer to tell you what she wants, what she needs and what she will pay. Only by finding these things out can you find a way to deliver products that please and help her.

If You Want To Catch Chickens Don't Dress Like a Fox

Let me digress here for a moment to talk about dress. The first rule is to dress so that you are physically comfortable. After all, you may be a little mentally uncomfortable when you start selling, so it will help to wear your favorite set of appropriate clothes. The key word is "appropriate." The second rule—and it's equally important—is that you should dress in a way that's acceptable within the company on which you are calling.

The San Francisco Bay Area has some of the country's largest banks and some of the world's hottest high-tech companies. Every one of those companies has its own corporate culture. One of the cameramen who works with me has said he could be blindfolded and put in any corporation's building. After removing the blindfold, he would be able to tell you what company he was at by the furniture and the manner in which people there dress. When I call on a prospect in a company I have not visited before, I often ask people who know for their advice about the way people dress there.

Know Something about the
Prospect's Company

Knowing how to dress is just one concern when planning your first appointment. Another thing to know that will help you—sometimes a little, sometimes a lot—is the overall business of the company on which you are calling; its size, scope and nature. Finding that information on larger publicly traded companies can be as easy as calling their public relations departments to get past annual reports. If you are calling on small or middle-market businesses, finding that information can be more of a challenge.

Again, trade magazines and periodicals can be a good place to look. Local newspapers often keep files of articles about the people and companies they report on. Some newspapers will allow people who ask politely to review those files. Larger local libraries sometimes have similar files available.

I found out about the clip files at our library when I got a cold call from a woman selling health insurance. She knew about some business I was awarded about a year before, and she also knew a little bit about my business. I was impressed that she knew even that much because my operation has a very low profile. She found an article which had run in the business section of the local paper that was based on a press release I sent out. The article was among the files at the local library.

Find Out about the Business

- Call its PR department for past annual reports.
- Scour trade magazines.
- Read the newspaper.
- Do library research or surf the Internet.

Another place to find out about a business is on the Internet. Many businesses—concerned that they'll be left at the information superhighway's on ramp—have home pages on the net. The benefit to you is that you may discover some useful information about a prospective client if her company has a home page.

Plan Your Questions—Ask about the:

- Prospect's personal goals
- Organization's goals
- Obstacles that prevent achieving those goals
- Operational issues about the unit
- Methods the unit uses to meet the company's business objectives

---

Before your appointment you also have to plan your list of questions to discover what the customer wants, needs and will pay. What kind of questions? Start with the same ones you asked or wanted to ask when you first talked to the prospect on the phone—questions about the prospect's personal goals and her organization's goals. Also, you should ask about things that would prevent her from meeting those goals, operational issues about her group and the way her work unit meets the company's business objectives.

Other questions will come to mind when you are waiting in the lobby or at the desk of your prospect. How? Look around for an employee magazine or for other internal communications. They may contain a lot of information about the current important topic or topics around the company.

Keep Your Eyes Open and Your Head on a Swivel

The foyer is also a good place to look for trade magazines about the prospect's industry, too. They give you an idea of industry trends and, most important of all, help you to speak knowledgeably to some of the prospect's industry-related concerns. If you appear to be more knowledgeable than your competitors, your prospect is more likely to become your client. Look for the subscription order forms that are often inside these magazines. Subscriptions to many of them are free.

**The Prospect's Environment
Yields Tons of Information**

Professional

- Internal communications like magazines and newsletters
- Industry-related trade magazines
- Company recognition
- Industry awards

Personal

- Pictures of family and friends
- Organized or disorganized
- Mementoes

Also keep an eye out for awards from inside or outside the company. They are kept in full view because people are proud of that recognition. Ask your prospect how the award was earned. Ask about the details of the project or unique aspects of it. If the award is a recent one, congratulate the person. And if you know something about the award, the project that earned it, or if someone told you something good about the project, bring it up during the course of the conversation.

Survey the prospect's surroundings. The environment will tell you a lot about that person and about the organization. If the person has a cluttered desk, the person is either really disorganized (a potentially bad sign) or has a million things going (a potentially good sign). The office environment is also a window to the person's personal life. Pictures of family or friends in particular activities can lead to questions like, "Is that your boat? How long have you enjoyed sailing/horses/golf? How often do you get a chance to enjoy it?"

How important are questions like that? Very, because they help break the ice.

For example, on my first visit with a woman who was responsible for a training program with a retailer, I noticed she had a picture of a Rhodesian Ridgeback dog on her desk. Since two of that breed are part of my family, I was quick to ask her where she got the dog. I discovered that she bought her dog from the same breeder as I bought mine. We spent about 15 minutes just talking about her dog, my dogs and the breeder before we got down to the business of discussing her project.

My conversation was based on genuine interest in something we had in common. It helped to make our conversation more casual. I know it made me feel more comfortable, and I would safely guess that it made her comfortable, too. In the end she awarded me the business, and I have continued to do work for her since.

Open with a Personal Touch and Then

Try to control the pace and progress of every meeting. Even so, remember that we are all different. Some people like to get right to the point, while others talk about anything *but* the business at hand. In that regard, some part of managing a meeting's progress is intuitive.

Typically, the personal part of the conversation comes at the beginning of the appointment. Of course, you don't want to appear to waste too much of your prospect's time, so be pleasant and cordial. Then, without rushing things, move the conversation toward business. That means: Thank the prospect for taking the time to see you and provide a *brief* overview about yourself. Your overview should reiterate the letter you sent her and give a little more detail about budget amounts, schedules, critical details or issues that you had to manage. You want to impress upon the prospect that you are a capable vendor.

Listen 80 Percent—Talk 20 Percent

Your next step is to begin the process of discovery about the prospect's responsibilities to her department and the department's responsibilities to the company. Imagine a funnel. Start by getting the big picture. As the meeting progresses, you can get more focused about her and the potential business she represents.

Whether you already know a little bit about the prospect's business or not, ask how the department fits into the company's organization chart. Ask how the department helps the company meet its business objectives. Ask how the department is funded within the company or how projects that the department undertakes are paid for.

In my business, for example, some companies require their internal video departments to charge back the entire cost of the project to the requesting department. If the video department can't get enough work to stay afloat, the people on staff don't have much job security. In some companies, departments charge only for out-of-pocket expenses. There are also other departments, though they are few in this day and age, that exist purely for the whim of the company.

Ask about the person's background, personal and professional. Where did she go to school? How did she wind up in this business? What kind of job did she have before the one she is currently in? How long has she been with this company? What other companies has she worked with? What does she like about the current job?

Don't make it sound like you're someone from personnel interviewing a job candidate. You are trying to find out as much as you can about the prospect and her department's way of doing business. That will help you find some common ground to begin building a personal relationship to get the business the prospect has to offer.

Ask About the Prospect's Vendors

- What do you expect from your vendors (in the way of performance, price or practices)?
- Can you tell me about some of the critical services that they deliver?
- If there was one thing you would have your vendors do differently, what would that be?

Ask questions about the vendors the prospect currently uses. Ask her what conditions need to exist or circumstances that must arise for her to use vendors. Ask about the prospect's expectations of the vendors' quality of work. By uncovering this information about the vendors the prospect currently uses, you will clarify two things. You will know if you have the skills to meet the prospect's needs. You will also know if the prospect can afford you.

After all, if you have a 2-person staff doing corporate law and your prospect currently has as 30-person firm on retainer, it is unlikely you will be able to support that company's legal requirements—unless you are highly specialized. Or, if you are a skilled graphic artist and the vendors which the prospect uses are fresh out of art school, odds are the vendors are getting paid entry level fees for their work. The prospect may not want to or may not be able to afford your work unless she is interested in increasing the quality of her department's work.

But there are more questions about the prospect's vendors that you need to ask. Those questions include, "What do the vendors you use do well? What are some of the projects you turn to them for? Why? How long have you worked with them?"

Asking the First Critical Question

Throughout this line of questioning about vendors, the prospect is going to reveal many things. She will tell you what level of work she wants, why and how much she is willing to pay for it. She will tell you the challenges she and her department face. That information will give you some idea about how you can fit in; you'll be helping her to meet and overcome those challenges. She may even talk about office politics or more.

There are three reasons to get her on track discussing vendors. The first is because of the general information you can glean. The second is to just get her comfortable talking about her vendors. The third is to set the stage to ask her the first of two very critical questions.

The first of those two questions is a delicate one. (We'll discuss the second question on page 99.) Phrase it carefully. It can open the door for you because in its answer lies the key. The question is: *"What can your current vendors do to improve their service to you?"*

If you ask it improperly, you imply, "If you aren't getting the service you need from these vendors, why do you continue to use them?" That can make the prospect look like an idiot. Try phrasing it this way, "If you could wave a wand to have everything perfect, what would you change in your vendor relationships?" The answer your prospect gives you will tell you what areas you can sell to—areas in which the prospect's vendors may have been falling short.

Don't conduct a personnel interview. You also don't want to conduct the interview like one of the late-night talk-show hosts. You know, the host asks a question like, "So, you have a new movie out, huh?" The guest answers, "Yes, but more importantly I am pregnant with the president's child." But while the guest answers, the host looks at his list of questions to ask another and doesn't hear the eye-popping announcement. Instead, the host asks, "Well, what was it like working in the Yukon during those cold winter nights?"

Listen to your prospect's responses. In fact, if you need to pause thoughtfully and jot a note between her response and your next question, so much the better. If you have your questions committed to memory, great.

Having done this for some years now, this part of the process has become pretty natural to me. Still, I like to pay attention to a prospect, how she responds, and I also like to survey her surroundings to look for hints of her personal tastes and pleasures. To ensure that I ask all of the questions I need to ask, I carry a list of them in my day planner all of the time.

You should create and carry a list of questions for your first visit with a prospect. It shows her that you have prepared for the meeting. It shows that you have a focus, an objective. It makes you appear professional and interested. Best of all, it frees you up to listen to your prospect and to take copious notes without having to worry about what the next question should be.

When the 80/20 Rule Changes

About one-half to two-thirds of the way through my meeting with a new prospect, I want to present my demo reel. If you have a portfolio of work that is important to show, make certain you do that. The general rule is that in the development stages of your relationship you should listen to the client 80 percent of the time and talk 20 percent. This is a part of the meeting where that rule changes. You will talk more than the prospect because you will be describing the projects you worked on, your role in them, the budgets it took to complete them, the complexities of the projects, and the obstacles or challenges to their success.

If you plan it properly, you will have spent the first half or more of the meeting discovering information about what the prospect wants, needs and will pay. That way, when you begin to discuss your reel or portfolio or other work samples, you can sell to those three areas. Best of all, if you have asked the first critical question, she should have revealed enough information about what she would like to change in her vendor relationships. Then you can also sell your skills based on what she would like to see differently in those relationships.

Don't Apologize for Earlier Work

One thing you absolutely should not do, however, is apologize for the work you have done. When I was on staff, people who called on me would sometimes say, "This could have been a better project, but the budget was too small," or, "We wanted to do thus and so, but we just didn't have the people who could help." What people were actually saying was, "I really underestimated how much it would take to pull that off," and "I don't know how to hire the right people for the projects I do."

A client who manages the video function for a retailing company told me about a woman who came in with over 20 years of experience and apologized for the lack of creativity in the work she was showing. My colleague told me that she certainly wouldn't hire that woman, and I don't blame her.

In any business, one of the keys to success—whether or not you are self-employed—is understanding the restrictions and limitations you face on a project and managing the project to eliminate or avoid potential problems. So instead of apologizing for a low budget, say things like, "We were able to do this for only $X. It was a challenge, but the client was very happy with the end product."

Clients and prospects want to hear only about good things because they want to have confidence in the people they hire. You have to build that confidence in them so they will give you the work. You can only do that with a string of successes behind you.

You hope your prospect will be interested enough in your work to ask questions about it. This is generally a good sign. I say generally because some people are just nice and ask all the right questions without ever expecting to hire you for anything. A truly good buying signal is when the prospect starts talking about similar projects her department has done. When that happens, both of you are building a common bond. If the prospect calls other people into the office to look at your work, things are obviously going very well for you.

Asking the Second Critical Question

After you spend about half an hour or so with your prospect, it is time to conclude the meeting. But there is still one more very important question. Ask the prospect if there are any projects in the foreseeable future on which you might be able to help.

That's right. You *ask for the business*.

You could say something like, "You mentioned the need for someone who can respond to tight deadlines or a short turn-around time. That one sample I showed you illustrates my ability to do just that. And I have other clients like Vector Intersections and GUI Graphics where I have done similar work quickly. Do you expect any project that needs someone with skills like mine in the immediate future?"

The manner in which the prospect responds will probably be enough to tell you whether or not you can expect to work with her. People have said to me, "No, but I am certain we will have a project for you soon. I would like to work with you." If the prospect is cool in his response to your question, you will know that you must find out why you didn't light the prospect's fire. That means you have further to go to discover what you need to do to get the prospect to look favorably on you.

Even with a prospect who calls in 15 people to pour over your sample materials, odds are very great that you will leave the first meeting without a project. Don't despair. If things have gone as they should, you truly have begun to build that long-term relationship.

However it goes, like any social situation, as your meeting concludes thank the prospect for his time and information. Tell him you'll stay in touch on a regular basis. If the prospect has asked to see additional work or needs references, promise to get back to him at a specific time, and make certain you follow through. Then skedaddle.

You have now made at least three impressions on this person—a letter, a phone call and a personal interview. If you originally met at a professional meeting or social gathering, then you've made four impressions. You are well on your way to doing business with him. You will make another impression with a thank-you letter or card after the meeting, and again if you need to follow up on a commitment made during your meeting. Some people I know like to leave their portfolios or demo reels behind so they have yet another chance to make an impression when they pick the samples up later.

Your job now is to stay in touch.

CHAPTER 9

Staying in Touch

Staying in touch is critical because you must continue to make positive impressions on the prospect and you can do so in a variety of ways. Send a pertinent article you have read and think the person might like. Include a personal note that tells about your current projects. If those projects are in the prospect's industry, or if they may even appear to meet the prospect's wants and needs, don't hesitate to convey that in your note, too.

The Personal Touch Can Pay Off

One thing I do annually is write Christmas cards, but I don't simply get some printed up, sign them with a wisp, stuff and address envelopes and mail them. I write personal notes to my clients and prospects.

If the recipient is a regular client I thank her for the relationship. I tell her how important the relationship is to me and how much I appreciate the work. I also include a comment about the person—something about her that I particularly like. For example, one of my best clients is different from the others because she expects so much more from me than the others. Her expectations make me work even harder, but the work turns out even better than I expect. So I have told her that.

If the recipient is a periodic client, I thank him for the opportunities he has given me, and I add that I hope we can work together again soon. I also add a personal comment.

If the recipient is a prospect, I tell her about some of the highlights I have enjoyed during the past year. I add that I hope to work with her in the upcoming year. If I can, I close with an appropriate personal comment.

I don't blow smoke. I don't write something I don't truly mean or believe. I don't gush, but I express all of it from the heart. Every card is handwritten. And, given the size of my Christmas card list, it is a lot of work. I usually start writing two to three cards a day in October and increase the number daily as necessary as December approaches. Then, two weeks before Christmas, I send them out all at once. I do that so if I am sending more than one to an office, everybody gets his or her card at the same time.

I started sending personal holiday greetings one year when I was looking at all of the impersonal greetings I was receiving. None contained more than a cursory handwritten greeting and signature. If just one person had taken the time to write something a little personal it would have stood out. That struck a chord with me, so I sat down and started to write.

The result was the busiest first quarter I ever had—typically the slowest quarter for me. And I had it during the midst of a deep recession. In one stretch I worked 35 of 40 days. Talking with a colleague about my busy period of work he said, "Well, I worked the other five."

Did I get work from every card I sent? No. And I didn't expect to. I simply wanted to do two things: To thank people for the opportunities they gave me and to tell people with whom I had yet to work that I looked forward to the chance. The people who did call to ask me to work for them all mentioned the card, however. Three said the card was well-timed because a project had just come up, and my holiday greeting made them think of me. As the adage goes, "Luck is simply being prepared to take advantage of opportunity."

Consider a "Satisfaction Guaranteed" Offer

Another stay-in-touch method I used may be only helpful when calling on a buyer with a retailing company. Try to adapt it to your situation.

Sales cycles in my business can be fairly long. Though many times I begin working with someone a few weeks or months after my initial contact with them, I anticipate anywhere from one to two years of steady contact with a prospect before he becomes a client. In one case, I had been calling on the manager of a video production unit in a retailing environment for about two years. He was always very cordial—that being defined as one who returns calls and spends time talking to help you further understand his wants and needs—but I just couldn't get him to ask me to bid on a project.

People are homeostatic. They tend to want to use someone they have used before, a proven performer. I am the same way.

In this situation I needed to figure a way to bump the prospect out of using the same people all of the time. He worked for a retailer with a very liberal refund policy. So I sent him a certificate guaranteeing him a complete refund of my fees if he was not 100 percent satisfied with what my company did for him, just as his company does with its customers. He appreciated the gesture, and he asked me to bid on the next project he had. We got the job, we were never asked for a refund, and we still work for that company today—even though he has moved on to other things.

Perhaps the offer might not have been effective if we had only been building the relationship a short while. I knew he was open to something different, and I knew the guarantee wasn't much of a risk for me. I simply had to prove to him that I wanted to and could meet his and his company's needs.

Offer To Be a Backup

A colleague and friend who went out on his own used a different method. He acknowledged up front that his prospects had their list of people to first call for help. He asked prospects to put him at the top of the call list if they had 11th hour work for which no other people were available. He got the work as he asked, and that gave him the opportunity to show his stuff. Needless to say, he quickly wound up on people's "A" list as one of the first to call.

Remember from Chapter 8 that only about 10 percent of people ever make enough calls on a prospect to get new business. Especially when just starting out, you need to persevere because virtually all of your new business will be coming from prospects that you converted into clients.

Is One Enough? Are Three Too Many?

Inevitably people ask one of two questions, "How many calls on a prospect is too many calls?" or "How often should I call on a prospect to stay in touch?" The short answers that are obviously not definitive are, "You can never call too many times," and "Call frequently enough that the prospect remembers you and your work, so that if there comes a time that she needs you, she'll at least consider calling."

Typically, after I have met with a prospect, I call at least once every six to eight weeks—or more often if I have a reason to call. For example, let's say a professional organization I am involved in needs a speaker or help in judging for a festival and I think a particular prospect can fill the bill. Then I call. If I am simply trying to arrange my first appointment with the prospect, I call until I either get the appointment or until I am told to stop calling. I have only been told to stop calling twice in nine years. Of course, sometimes people don't ever return my call.

There is a major apparel manufacturer in my area which does a lot of video production. Having been referred to them by one of the directors of photography who works for me, I sent the department head my introductory letter. I followed the letter up with my call. No response. So I called again in a few days. No response. I called a third time several days after that. No response. I called my friend who referred me. He told me that the prospect was notorious for letting her voice mail pick up all of her calls and for not returning calls—even to those who are involved in a project for her.

Because I believe that a person can't have too many good vendors, I feel it is my duty to show them my work so they can hire me. This situation was no different. I knew I could do the work for this prospect. Though I was aware that she already had a stable of people working for her, I also knew that—as with my other current clients—sooner or later she would need someone else. So I continued to call her, along with sending letters when I had something I thought she might find interesting. Faithfully. Once a week for 52 weeks. She never returned my phone calls.

Why did I continue to call? She never told me to stop calling. Wasn't it a waste of my time? In hindsight you might think so. Was I afraid of becoming a pain in the behind? No. You see, you will not get the business unless you ask for it. As far as wasting my time, well, there was always a momentary lull in the action when I could fit in a phone call.

But 52 weeks in a row! Doesn't that verge on violation of stalking laws? Possibly, but I know one writer who finally got work after two years of weekly calls to someone at Apple Computer. I told my story to one of my clients. She said she would have hired me simply for working so hard to get to see her.

Stay in the Prospect's Mind

The point is, you need to stay in the prospect's mind until the prospect needs you. Along the way, you need to give her one or more significant reasons to hire you. You don't want to spend your time and energy sending someone a letter, getting an appointment, meeting with them, even sending them a proposal and then being forgotten about. That happened to me, and I vowed it would never happen again.

I called on one of the country's largest wineries for about a year. As with other prospects, I sent an introductory letter to the person whom I thought would buy services like mine; in this case, it was the winery's marketing director. She referred the letter to a subordinate who would be responsible for internally managing the video project. The subordinate and I spoke over the phone periodically for several months. The winery wanted a videotape about the winery to play in the tasting room.

After a couple of letters to the subordinate, along with at least a half dozen phone calls, he invited us to the winery for our first meeting to present our capabilities. The meeting went well. But because they were still working out budget details, they weren't quite ready for a proposal. I continued to build the relationship, staying in touch with him and with the people we met that day at the winery.

Finally, after about a year, my contact asked for a proposal. I asked if he had a specific budget amount planned for the project, and he told me $25,000 to $30,000.

Remember that in order to get business you need to know what someone wants, what someone needs and what someone is willing to pay. From my meetings and phone calls, I had a good idea of what the winery needed, and he just told me what they could afford. So I was two-thirds of the way to getting new business. Now I just needed to give him what he wanted.

Arriving for the meeting at which I would present the proposal, I followed a late-model Mercedes Benz into the parking lot. My prospect climbed out from behind its steering wheel. He was wearing a beautiful cashmere sport coat. On the way to his office, I also noticed he was wearing a Rolex watch. When we got in his office I saw the richly appointed details there. Not surprisingly, his office walls wore gorgeous photography of the vineyards, the winery and the wines they made there. The point is that this guy was not afraid of spending money on himself or the winery.

We made our way through the proposal that detailed the project's objective, the target audience, the concept, the project time line and the budget. I added what I felt was a nice twist to it by showing him how he could actually have the video pay for itself. He seemed pleased with the presentation.

When I was finished, I asked him what other companies were bidding on the project. He mentioned a second company that I periodically found myself competing against, a worthy adversary because the company had a strong sales staff, but they also had high overhead. I explained that my overhead was significantly lower, and that allowed for more of the client's money to wind up on the screen than if the winery went with the competitor.

Then he pushed a single piece of paper across the desk. It was the bid/proposal from a third company. He asked me what I thought of it.

I looked at it. There were no details listed, save specific deliverables like how many days they would shoot, how big the crew was going to be and how much editing they planned to do. At the bottom of this one-page bid was the competitor's estimated cost: $2,900.

I thought to myself, "This competitor is obviously too low, and they don't appear to know what they are doing. It looks like it's between me and the other guys." Then I looked up and said, somewhat smugly, "It looks like they dropped a zero from the left of the decimal."

"No," the marketing guy said. "That's their bid."

I said, "When I do proposals for the Department of Defense, a bid like this wouldn't make the first cut because it doesn't conform to the bid specifications. It reflects a lack of understanding about the client's needs." Then I put the bid back on the marketing guy's desk and wrapped things up. I asked him when we could start the project (remember to always ask for the business). He said that he was still considering all three proposals, but he promised a decision in a week. I expected to hear that we were awarded the new project. After all, I knew that we gave the winery what they needed, what they were willing to pay and what they wanted.

I was wrong. They awarded the job to the company with the single-page, $2,900 bid. They bought something that was a lot less than what they could afford. They were willing to make a decision based on price. They wanted something for less cost than what I or the other competitor offered.

It was hard not to take the loss of that business personally because I had worked so hard on the proposal. I worked hard for a year just to get asked to develop and deliver the proposal. I felt as though I had been jilted by a lover.

The best way to forget about someone is to find someone else. So that's what I did. To my chagrin. It hurt too much thinking about the business someone else got and that I felt I had earned, so I didn't stay in touch with the people at the winery. The other competitor that didn't win the bid was smarter, though, because one of its sales representatives did stay in touch. When it became obvious that the $2,900 bidder couldn't deliver, the winery's marketing guy needed someone in a hurry to fill in. He turned to the people who had stayed in contact with him—my other competitor on the project.

You never truly fail if you learn from your experiences. I certainly learned from that one. I began to diligently stay in touch with clients and prospects.

One of my earliest independent projects was for a regional bank. Even though they did very few projects, I stayed in touch with my contact there—the head of the communications department. One day I bumped into her at the airport. We exchanged pleasantries and headed off to our respective departure gates. About a month later she called to ask me to meet about a possible project. We did, and in the process I met one of her subordinates (a "real" buyer) whose responsibilities had grown to include managing the bank's video projects.

The job was awarded to another company, but I continued to stay in touch with both people. Several months later, they called me in to do a rush project—without having to enter into a competitive bidding process.

The moral of the story is obvious. Once you have built the relationship—regardless of what happens in the interim—*stay in touch*.

CHAPTER 10

Asking the Right Questions and Avoiding Red Flags

So, your diligence has paid off. You've stayed in touch, and your prospect just asked you to develop a proposal. Finally, you get a shot at doing what it is you like to do. Good for you. But before you get too excited, let's talk a little bit about the down side of requests for proposals, or RFPs.

It doesn't happen often, but now and then I get asked for proposals that don't have a snowball's chance of getting me work. Almost always these requests come from people I have not been calling on. I don't seem to get these requests as often as I used to. I think that, to a certain degree, my increased experience in qualifying and recognizing real buyers has helped reduce these "make work" proposals. The big downside to working on requests that keep you busy but not billing is that you are not out talking to actual buyers.

If you are just starting out, and your proposal development and presentation skills are weak, it may be to your benefit to answer all requests for proposals. Also, regardless of the requestor's motivation, you will get seen.

If your proposal development and presentation skills are up to par, then try to avoid requests for proposals that bear one of the following red flags.

Red Flag #1: "Don't Work Too Hard on This"

When a prospect says something like, "Don't work too hard on this proposal," he probably means that he has already selected another vendor for the project, but his boss wants him to get three bids. On the other hand, this is the one red flag RFP that you have a shot at, because it *is* a competitive situation, because he might have to show his boss the three proposals and because his boss might be the real buyer. If you do create a proposal, give it your best effort.

Red Flag #2: "Just Curious—How Much Will This Cost?"

"I'm just calling around to get an idea of how much it will cost" is the opening line of a conversation that usually bears no fruit. In my first couple of months of self-employment, the owner of a small advertising agency called me to his office to talk about a project for his client—a hospital.

As I sat on his sofa, he said, "I'm just curious how much it would cost to do the project." His request seemed benign enough. Besides, I needed and wanted the work. I had the good sense to tell him that I could figure a firmer cost after going back to my office to work out the details.

"No, no," he insisted. "I'm just curious what it would take." He continued to press for a couple of more minutes while I hemmed and hawed. I finally broke down and gave him a high ball-park estimate, underscoring that it *was* a high ball-park figure. I reiterated that I could give him a true estimate of costs once I returned to my office to work out the numbers.

What did he say? You probably have already guessed. "That's okay. I can get it done for a couple of thousand dollars cheaper." I didn't get the work.

Now, I never give a cost estimate for a project off the top of my head unless I know the client very well. Even then, I add a strong caveat that I need to run a real estimate when I get back to the office. I recommend that you follow that same policy. Even if you know your client well when you give your estimate, you set yourself up for trouble if you don't really consider all of the project's elements. If you figure too low, you might be stuck for the extras you forgot to consider. If you figure too high, you might look like you are gouging the client, and that can jeopardize your relationship. Worse, it could drive the client to ask another vendor for a bid. If you casually estimate the cost of a project you will casually *not* get the business.

Red Flag #3: "I'm Just Calling for My Boss"

Another red flag is a variation of "I'm just calling for my boss to see what the costs are." It could also be, "We're just looking for some ideas." These are *always* telephone inquiries from people who don't actually have any authority to make a decision about the project. Often these people work for a boss who is a hands-on manager but who refuses to participate in the decision-making meetings or delegate the project. These requests can consume a lot of your time—time you may find difficult, if not impossible, to bill for.

When an assistant calls "just to get an idea of numbers for the boss," I explain that it would be like a contractor giving an estimate on building a house without asking the appropriate questions and without drawing up the appropriate plans. Unless I know where the person wants to build the house, what amenities the person wants to fill the house with and so on, I can't honestly tell her what I think it will cost to build it. So, I need to ask a lot of questions.

Then, I pull out my list of questions and begin asking them. The red flag is definitely up when the assistant can't answer my questions. "But I really just want to get an idea of the cost," he says.

I gently reiterate that I would be better able to give him an idea of costs once I got the answers to just a few specific questions. Then I offer to meet with the person for half an hour at no charge. I even offer to send him the questions to which I need answers. If he agrees to getting answers and then meeting with me, then I know I have a shot at some business. If not, then his call is not worth my time, and I may as well hang up.

I have also gotten this kind of call from a few less-than-scrupulous competitors who are trying to find out how much

I charge for various kinds of work. As a rule, I am willing to talk about my business and business practices with people who ask. I feel strongly that there is enough business out there for all competent and capable people to earn a good living, and I know I am going to get my share of work. If someone is up front about wanting my expertise, I am glad to help.

Red Flag #4: The Shotgun RFP

Depending on your business, you may find it useful to be listed in a professional directory. I am in several directories simply because of my affiliations with some professional organizations. I have found that if I am getting called because of one of those listings, many other people are too.

Someone once called asking for a bid for a half-hour infomercial. It was a simple request that came via my voice mail. "We are interested in producing a half-hour program. Please fax your costs to—"and she left her fax number. We passed.

Government RFPs

One other place where I have had a chance to develop proposals but haven't generated much business success is with the local, state and federal governments. Some people make a very good living working as independent suppliers to government agencies. To me, bidding on government projects is kind of like playing the lottery. Sooner or later somebody is going to win, but how about those odds?

I personally find it difficult relating to an organization that doesn't operate on the principle of making a profit. Corporations are responsible to shareholders to do that. The people who work in those corporations seem to understand that vendors need to make a profit to stay in business.

On top of the paperwork that's involved in bidding on government work, government agencies make the bidding open to a large number of companies. These agencies also try to make the process at least appear fair. The result? Like most things in life that are controlled by government agencies, the process can be quite complicated and very often unwieldy.

In my early days of self-employment, I got listed with the federal government as a "qualified supplier." Our local library received and maintained a listing of thousands of federal requests for proposals for a myriad of different projects. Because it was an easy place to look for work, I went to review the weekly posting.

None of my proposals bore any fruit until we wrote one for an interactive video wall for the Army Corps of Engineers. Not only were we the lowest bidder, we were the only bidder to meet one critical requirement—not to exceed $100,000.

We met with the negotiator and two principals who were the project's managers. At the meeting they told us to cut our bid by another 15 percent or we wouldn't get the work! Having written the bid with a very sharp pencil, I knew we had no fat to cut. The RFP asked to include five language versions—English, French, German, Spanish and Japanese. The translations and process for including the five languages in the video wall were going to cost about $15,000. So I suggested that they cut that requirement. "Nope," they said. They weren't interested. They kept the specs the same, but they still wanted me to cut our bid by 15 percent.

I pointed out that we were the only company that found a way to do the job for the "not to exceed" amount. The negotiator didn't care. We went back and forth for over a week. I finally decided not to accept the project because I couldn't reduce the budget unless they cut some of their requirements.

As a policy we no longer bid on government projects. But that means there is one less competitor for those who do bid. Somebody is going to get the business. Will it be you?

You may find yourself in one of these situations doing a lot of work for a little or no return. But don't misunderstand. In the early days of my business, I developed several proposals that had no chance of paying off. I wasn't as busy then as I am now, and I found it worthwhile because my proposals and presentation skills improved with the practice. Both are important to getting business and important to staying successfully self-employed. Remember the story in Chapter 1 about the African lion that had to learn to eat before it got eaten?

> ### You Must Discover:
>
> - What the prospect wants
> - What the prospect needs
> - What the prospect will pay
>
> ### Then Discover:
>
> - The prospect's expectations of the finished product

Determining Your Prospect's Expectations

Your interviews and phone conversations with the prospect and the research you did along the way help you begin to develop a relationship with that person. Most important of all, you are well on your way to understanding what the client needs, what the client wants and what the client will pay.

If you charted those three things on a graph, you'd find that they practically never intersect. Because they often don't jibe, you must also determine what the client's expectations are of the finished project. To have a good shot at getting the business you then need to ask yourself, "Does what the client expect me to deliver match what I am going to deliver?" If the answer is no, then you need to review what your prospect has told you. You may need to talk with the prospect some more.

I once produced a video for a client to use in a series of trade shows. By design, it was only useful in a trade show environment, but it was highly received so the client asked me for a proposal to adapt the program to use as a stand-alone sales tool. Of course, I was glad to do that.

Knowing how much they paid for the trade show booth and the video presentation, I felt pretty certain about what the company could afford. I also felt intimately knowledgeable about what the client wanted because I had already spent a significant amount of time working with her to develop the trade show video.

We created four treatments. The estimates to produce them ranged from $40,000 to $60,000—not a squanderous amount of money for a video of its type. My client absolutely loved two of the four treatments. She went to get her boss to help decide which concept was best for the company and to discuss the costs associated with producing either of them.

Her boss liked the ideas, too, but he *didn't* like the costs. In fact, he had hoped to only spend between $5,000 and $15,000— significantly less than they spent on the trade show project and significantly less than any of my concepts. So with a new understanding of how much the client's boss really wanted to spend, I went back to the drawing board. We developed two other proposals based on the much more modest budget restrictions.

After I presented the less expensive proposals, he kept looking at them saying, "If we could only get something more exciting for less money." I wanted to tell him that there's always phone sex but I didn't. Instead, I described what it would take to do the work—my effort and that of my vendors, along with the other expenses that the project would incur. He continued to ask if we could do more for less. In the end, he wanted way more product than he was willing to pay for, and I walked away from the work.

Originally, I felt certain that we would get the business. I thought I had all of my ducks in a row. I just didn't know what my client's boss really expected for me to deliver. I am not certain he knew either. As a result, I spent a lot of time doing work, but not getting any in the end.

Which brings up another critical point. You have to know how much it costs you to do business. You have to know when to walk away from the table. Otherwise, your business can become a very costly hobby.

To Get Business Ask Questions

You will not get every bit of business you shoot for, but you can keep your odds high if you understand what the prospect wants, needs and will pay, as well as the end product the prospect expects. The best way to do that is to ask questions.

As I said, I keep a list of questions in my day planner so that if a client begins talking about a project I can ask the critical questions I think are necessary to uncover that information. The questions I ask are included in the client checklist on page 117. Obviously, adapt the list to your own style and industry.

Use the analogy of building a house to get the prospect to understand that it is necessary to ask questions in order to give her an accurate project estimate. By asking questions similar to "How big do you want it to be? What kind of fixtures do you want? What kind of floor covering?" and so on, you will also get the prospect to think a little harder about her project and be even more specific about the project's requirements. Best of all, such questioning increases the likelihood for you to bid successfully on the project because you'll better understand how the client perceives the end product. Also, getting the prospect to give specific answers to these questions greatly increases the likelihood for a successful project.

When you ask these questions, don't be afraid to ask them again in a different way or to ask them several times. When the client responds, reiterate what you have heard. In short, communicate, communicate, communicate.

How the Questioning Process Can Build Your Business

Once I got a call from a woman representing a company based in Minnesota. This company's business consisted of putting on professional conferences around the country. They were producing one in San Francisco for corporate trainers. When she called, my first question was how she had heard about my company. She said the president of a local trade group I belong to recommended me along with two of my competitors. It was obvious to me that she was not "just getting an idea of costs."

She told me that besides producing conferences, the company sells training and motivational materials and publishes a trade magazine. She also said that they were considering a new venture—producing and selling videotapes on training-related subjects. To test the waters, her company figured that, since

The Client Checklist

1. What are the primary issues we want the program to cover?
2. What is (are) the overall goal(s) we want to achieve?
3. What objectives need to be met to achieve the above goal?
4. What do you want viewers to think, feel or do after they watch this program?
5. How will we know that the objectives are achieved?
6. Who is the audience?
7. What is the current attitude toward this subject matter?
8. What is the knowledge of the target audience about this subject matter?
9. What is the environment in which this program will be used?
10. What are the resources (which your department or company can make) available for this project?
11. What obstacles might impede the progress or prevent the success of the project?
12. What will be the monetary effect of the program on the department or company? Will it make money? Will it save money? If so, how much, when and why?
13. What is the anticipated or allocated budget for this project?
14. What is your personal stake in this program?
15. Who will be the authority on the program's content?
16. Who is the one person who has final approval?
17. What is the due date (drop dead date for critical uses)?
18. How will the program's distribution be handled?

they had several noted speakers during general sessions, they should set up some cameras in the hotel's grand ballroom to record the presentations. She said they also wanted to interview the speakers elsewhere in the hotel afterwards and to include those interviews in the finished tape.

After concluding our conversation, I put an estimate together. It included a very good portable television control room that had been used on over 100 productions of a comedy series. Crew, lights, set-up time, tape stock, a special lens: It all added up pretty quickly. I sent the budget estimate back to her and she quickly responded.

"We've got to cut this way, way down," she said. She told me that the project was still a test for them and that the company hadn't established a price point for the tapes. In fact, she wasn't convinced that people would even buy them. I began to understand her needs even more because I better understood what she wanted. My understanding led me to ask her more questions.

I discovered that she was willing to forgo the additional camera set-up for the interviews after the speakers' presentations. Instead we could interview them in the grand ballroom once people cleared out. I also discovered that she didn't care if we had a very tight shot of the speaker from the back of the ballroom, and we didn't need to record the graphics that were projected on a big screen either. So we cut the special long lens and a technical system to help us record the graphics. With a pencil sharpened by even better information—a result of more thorough understanding—I calculated a new budget that was half of my original estimate. In anyone's math, a 50 percent reduction is cutting things "way, way down."

But not quite enough, or so she said in her next conversation with me. They needed to cut it another 10 percent.

Generally, when I do a budget, I wind up with even more questions. In my business, virtually everything I do is a prototype. I mean, I never did exactly that project before. And prototypes are always more expensive than a mass-produced product because you need contingency plans. The more you can eliminate the need for contingencies, the tighter your budget can be.

So, by talking with her and asking her questions, I was able to eliminate other contingencies I had planned for. The result? Another client relationship was established, and we did the work.

To reiterate for the umpteenth time, you must build a relationship with the prospect so that you understand what she wants, needs and will pay, and to understand how she perceives the end product on which you have been asked to bid. The only way to build that relationship—to gain that understanding—is to ask questions.

Once you have done that, it is time to create your proposal.

CHAPTER 11

Creating Your Proposal

Having met with the prospect, asked all of your questions and done the necessary research, now you get to put your proposal together. You're moving ever closer to being successfully self-employed.

When I was on staff, I developed proposals and cost estimates, but the success of those proposals did not have a direct effect on my income. My department was a cost-center, and we were there at the convenience of the company. If I didn't get the project, I would still get the paycheck—a critical difference between working for a company and working for yourself.

Because the proposal stage is crucial to finally landing the business and, ultimately, getting paid for what I do, I put a lot of effort into the development of my proposals—even if it is for a long-term client. Of course, putting a lot of effort into a proposal doesn't ever guarantee getting the work. Remember my unsuccessful experience with the winery?

I try to develop a proposal that will be clearly understood even if it is read by someone in senior management who may be responsible to approve the expenditure but who may not know much about the project or my business. It is not unusual for one of my clients to send my proposal to executives with a copy of her budget request to get the necessary approvals. My

120

proposals are so clear and the milestones so detailed that even the corporate attorneys who create the contract lift wording right from them.

The proposal is important in another way, as well. It helps to clarify what I understand the project's parameters are and to set the client's expectations of what I plan to deliver.

The Eight Elements of a Proposal

So what should be in a proposal? As with the questions on my client checklist (see page 117), you will need to adapt this information to your industry. Of course, any proposal should be easy to read and easy to understand. If you are not a great writer, find someone to edit your proposals. You should still write them yourself, because it will help you more thoroughly understand the project. An editor provides another perspective and can be a valuable sounding board.

My wife often reads my proposals and gives me important feedback. If she doesn't understand what I am trying to say or do, she lets me know.

My proposals have eight elements:

1. Background/Overview
2. Project Objective(s)
3. Target Audience Description
4. Concept or Concepts
5. Schedule or Time Line
6. Costs/Materials
7. Key People on the Project
8. Information about You and Your Company

Let's discuss each of them.

Background/Overview

My proposals begin by briefly providing background information and an overview of the environment that makes the project necessary. It justifies the money and effort the company will spend on the project to any busy executive whose approval is a must. It also helps me to clarify my own understanding of the situation and to illustrate my understanding of the project for the client.

Project Objective(s)

A difficult thing for many people—client or vendor—is to appropriately describe any project's objectives. Near the end of my tenure with the bank, somebody from the marketing department gave us a two-page, single-spaced list of objectives for a ten-minute marketing videotape! Objectives shouldn't take more than a couple of sentences. If you can't boil the project's objectives down to that, either you need to get your client to focus better or you really don't understand the project and have little chance of getting the work.

Target Audience

Another couple of sentences in the proposal describe the intended target audience—the people who are going to do, feel, see or otherwise be affected by the work. For example, if a video's target audience consists of young people with only a high school education the program will take one direction. If the video is aimed at highly-paid, well-educated executives, it will take another direction. Describing the target audience accurately is critical because it also helps bring clarity to the project's proposal.

The Concept

The background, overview and target audience set the stage for the concept or concepts presented in the proposal. Those three sections explain the logic on which the concept is built.

I try to present a very detailed concept because it is the client's first look at the "house" we intend to build for her. That allows me to generate a very tight cost estimate of the project, and it helps me plan a realistic schedule.

Schedule or Time Line

You want to detail the project's time line for three reasons. First, you want to illustrate for your client that you know what it will take to meet her needs. Second, the schedule's demands will also have an effect on the project's budget one way or the other. Third, you need to know the impact that the project will have on your work with your other clients.

A schedule also helps to red-flag potential problems that a deadline creates. For example, a client wanted to make a videotape about the company's sexual harassment policy, and the deadline for delivering the program was less than a month away. I pointed out that the subject matter would very likely require a variety of senior executives to sign off on the script. The sign-off process would likely hinder completing the project on time.

He said he understood, but the deadline was the deadline. I agreed to the project, but in my proposal I described the potential problem again when I outlined the project's schedule. He appreciated that and used it as leverage to get people to give the project their utmost attention. There were still some delays, but the project was completed very quickly because he was able to get people's attention using the caveat about the schedule in my proposal.

The Budget

The budget is generally the thing the client is most interested in. In meetings when I present proposals, it seems that I spend more time talking about budget issues than I do about anything else.

Of course, the estimate is often based on certain assumptions I have made about the job, and I list those just below the bottom line. It is important to list those assumptions.

For example, the client may have mentioned that her internal graphics department will contribute to the project with graphic design. Spell that out as an assumption in your estimate, because if the graphics department can't come through as promised, someone will have to pay to get the project's graphics created. If it's listed as an assumption up front, there shouldn't be a problem later if you go back for a change order.

If your projects involve more than just your time, never generate a budget without using some software program as an aid. I still use the budget estimating template that I created when I started my business. It lists all of the elements I *might* need to produce a project. I start from the top and work my way down. It includes things like sales tax, which in California can add over 8 percent to the cost of an item or service.

The other thing the budget template does is help me look back at the project after it is completed. I review my estimated costs versus actual costs to see where I was too low or too high.

This is an important step, so don't overlook reviewing your project expenses afterwards. If I regularly estimate too high, I stand the risk of losing business to competitors simply because I am more expensive. If I regularly estimate too low, I stand the risk of going out of business because I am not meeting my overhead or other expenses.

The Importance of Overhead

Speaking of overhead, don't forget to include it in your budget. After about six months in business for myself, I was wrapping up a project. I spent a beautiful summer day processing my vendors' invoices and reviewing the project. As the day ended, it dawned on me that I just spent one entire day closing down the project, and I had not factored that into my budget. In essence, I worked on the project for free that day. Later during the tax season when I was sending out 1099 forms to vendors who worked on that and other projects, I realized that I was continuing to work for free. In addition to the back-office work, I realized I had to account for other office expenses like postage, phones, computers, insurance and so on. I adjusted my spreadsheet to begin including overhead in my project estimates.

Add a Contingency—Or a Profit

Another part of the budget that is important to include is the contingency. I have always factored in a contingency on project estimates—even when I was on staff. Now I look at the contingency as my profit margin. If I make a mistake on the project or if I didn't plan for all of the expenses in it and eat into the contingency, it's on me. Otherwise, the contingency becomes my profit. Though I make absolutely certain to meet or exceed my client's expectations, you can be assured that I work very hard to keep the contingency untouched.

On a couple of occasions some time back, however, clients asked me at the conclusion of the project if there was any money left over in the contingency. Because the projects had gone smoothly, it was obvious that they expected that I wouldn't charge as much. Since I listed a contingency, it seemed fair to them to ask. Now, I still list the contingency, but I call it *profit*. No one has had a problem since then, because clients understand that a business needs to make a profit to stay in business.

Key People

If the project requires that you hire key people with particular expertise, you should list them, too, along with background information about them. This is another way to illustrate that you know what it takes to do the work and that you have the resources to get the job done. If you have had prior experience working as a team with your experts, especially on a job similar to the one you are proposing, make certain to spell that out.

Information about You and Your Company

Finally, whether you are working with others on the project or if you are working alone, describe how your own professional expertise is perfect for the project. You may have been told all of your life that you shouldn't brag about yourself. Forget that now. You want the job. Brag. Make them want to hire you.

```
┌──────────────────────────────────────────┐
│       What Kind of Information Should      │
│              You Include?                  │
│                                            │
│   • List awards.                           │
│   • Describe or provide samples of sim-    │
│     ilar successful projects.              │
│   • List your current clients.             │
│   • Include other applicable work.         │
│   • Provide other relevant material.       │
└──────────────────────────────────────────┘
```

This section isn't a resume, but it contains similar information. For example, list the professional awards you have earned during your career. Describe one or more successful projects that were similar to the one you are proposing. Include a list of current clients. If you are just starting out, list some pro bono projects you worked on outside of the cozy corporate confines you used to enjoy.

This section can help your client justify to her boss why you were hired. I often say, only slightly tongue-in-cheek, this part of the proposal will help the client keep her job if you blow yours. If her boss asks her why things went to hell in a hand basket, she'll be able to point to all of the qualifications listed in that part of the proposal and say, "He's won awards for similar projects before. And look at his client list. I just don't know why he went bad on this project, but you can rest assured that I'll never hire him again!"

If it's appropriate, include samples of similar work for similar clients, along with descriptions of or explanations about the work. That might include the project's budget, the deadline, and other limitations, challenges or unique aspects about that project. For example, if you went to Asia to do a job and this project requires experience working in an Asian country, tell the client about this applicable experience.

Include whatever else might positively influence the decision to hire you, too. For example, I have written for or been interviewed by trade magazines about producing interactive projects—programs that combine video and computers so that the viewer can control what he wants to see. When I submit a proposal to a client who wants to do an interactive project, I include articles that I have written or for which I have been interviewed. This lends credence to my position as an expert, and helps to convince the client of that. It may also justify hiring me instead of someone else who charges less.

Once you've developed your proposal, you're ready for the next step in being successfully self-employed: Making the presentation.

CHAPTER 12

Making a Successful Presentation

Given all of your effort to get to this point, it is only fitting that you put an equal amount of effort into this stage of your relationship building. Make certain that you deliver the proposal in person.

So many people seem to be conditioned to faxing proposals to their clients. I think they are nuts. Presenting the proposal in person shows your commitment to the project. It also ensures that the prospect gives the proposal her personal and thorough attention.

Be Familiar with the Proposal

You should be so familiar with the proposal that you could give it verbatim by memory. You should also be able to answer any questions the prospect or his colleagues have about the proposal.

A mentor developed a significant proposal for an interactive television project. Much of the concept was still a lot of vapor, primarily because the technology to deliver the service was still being created.

Well, the big guys from Hollywood came up to see a sample we created based on this great idea. My mentor's boss's boss was also in the meeting. Impressed by the potential of the concept, one of the bigwigs from Tinseltown asked what it would cost to implement the plan. My mentor gave an honest answer: He said that there were still many details that needed to be worked through, and that because of the intricacies of the required technology he would need to do more research. He would, however, have the financial answer soon. The boss's boss—never known for having a gentle demeanor—exploded, abusively chiding my mentor in front of a roomful of people. In fact, it got to the point where everyone was embarrassed for the screaming idiot.

As embarrassing as it was for everyone, my mentor should have had some tentative numbers. To this day he never goes into a meeting without solid cost estimates under his arm and in his head, and neither do I.

Look Good To Look Good

One cosmetic issue. Get the proposal bound or made to appear presentation-like in some way. You can do that at your local copy store. It's cheap, and it adds a professional, finishing touch to your proposal. While you are at it, get four copies bound. That way you will have one for yourself and three for your prospect. If other people drop in on the meeting, you will look prepared. So will your prospect, and it never hurts to make your prospect look good.

Presenting the Proposal

Whether or not it really is true that 90 percent of genius is just showing up on time, absolutely don't be late to any meeting or job. This is an even more absolute rule when you are asking for the business.

To prevent being late, leave early for your appointment. That way, you will probably overcome just about anything that will happen.

My experience with the company from Minnesota that put on a conference in San Francisco is a good example. But it wasn't a presentation I was making, it was doing the actual job.

We set up in the grand ballroom of the hotel the day before the conference. Nearly everything was in place. To keep the costs way, way down, I was renting two videotape recorders from a vendor who couldn't give them up until the day of our shoot. So I had to pick them up from his office early that morning.

We didn't need to roll tape until 10:30 in the morning, so I had plenty of time to be leisurely about everything. In fact, I thought the start time was great because I'd be able to avoid the commuter rush going into the city.

After picking up the recorders, I decided to buck the traffic anyway just to make certain everything was going to be in order. As I neared the city I encountered a significantly greater amount of traffic than normal. The radio reports didn't give any clue about what was causing the backup. To my growing horror, traffic was nearing a dead stop—complete gridlock. Fortunately, I knew of some frontage roads that were worth trying so I altered my course. Nothing like having a plan to divert from, eh?

Somehow I was able to wend my way around much of the gridlock by taking frontage roads for a couple of exits, but I came to one spot where only the freeway could get me closer to my destination. To the consternation of those who were obeying California's traffic laws I sneaked over onto the emergency shoulder to keep moving. At the same time I saw the problem up ahead. It was an eight-car pileup with a number of emergency vehicles attending to it. Nobody was going anywhere. As soon as I saw the problem, the traffic reporter on the radio said the road would be blocked for at least another hour, perhaps even longer.

My mouth dried from anxiety. My crew at the hotel could do the work without me, but without the videotape recorders that I had they couldn't record the conference. Without recording the conference, I would eat the entire cost of the day. Frantically, I started hammering away on my cellular phone, but it was too early for any of my vendors on the other side of the accident to be in the office.

I could barely breathe. Then, as if Moses parted the traffic for me, I was able slip off the freeway and get right back on just past the accident.

The trip into the city normally takes less than an hour. That day it took me two and one-half hours. I got to the conference with about half an hour to spare. My engineer installed the machines before the break even began, and we all lived happily ever after.

No one plans to be late, but things happen that delay us. Leave for your meeting with plenty of time to avoid being breathless when you arrive, and so that you can concentrate on the important issue of getting the business.

Again, Keep Your Eyes Open and Your Head on a Swivel

As you did when you arrived for your first and subsequent meetings with the prospect, look around. Has anything changed? Scan the internal communications to glean any changes in corporate policy or anything that might have a bearing on your proposed project.

If you have time, review your presentation again. If you start to get nervous, remember that you can only get a hit if you are at the plate swinging. Besides, the worst possible thing that can happen is that you won't get the job. Now and again there will be times when getting the job will seem worse than not getting the job.

Try To Stay Calm

Just try to do your best during your presentation. In the movie *Unforgiven*, one gunfighter said that the winner of the gunfight isn't necessarily going to be the one who can draw first. It will probably be the one who stays calm enough during the fight to aim well. If you have prepared properly, then all you need to do is do the best you can. Stay as calm as you can to aim well. Remember that your competition may be just as nervous—or more—than you are.

During the Meeting

Be as enthusiastic about your proposal and the project as your personality will allow. Take notes, when appropriate, during the meeting. Answer questions succinctly. Absolutely do not hesitate to ask questions if something the client says is unclear.

The Most You Can Do Is the Best You Can

Gretchen Hirsch of the Stevens/St. John Company admitted that she gets nervous before every presentation. How does she overcome that nervousness?

"I just bomb right ahead. What's the worst thing they could say? 'No.' I like to concentrate on what's the best thing that can happen? The best thing that can happen is that I get a bigger order than I expected. The worst thing that can happen is that I don't get the project this time."

A critical challenge for you during the meeting is to uncover any spoken or unspoken objections or concerns the client has. If the client is straightforward, you probably will not have to probe for those issues. But people aren't always open enough.

Pay Attention to the Prospect's Body Language

Because people aren't always open verbally, you need to pay attention to things like body language. There are a variety of books available for you to learn about body language. Though nothing is absolute, there are a few key things to look for.

Facial expressions can be the most obvious. A frown or scowl or pursed lips are dead giveaways to a bothered client. A head nodding up and down is a good sign; one shaking back and forth isn't. If the prospect is stroking her chin she may be confused about something. If the prospect is leaning back with her arms and legs tightly folded, she is probably not receptive to the information you are conveying. If she is leaning forward and asking questions, she is probably more receptive to what you have to say.

Anticipate Objections and Prepare for Them

Try to anticipate possible objections and to prepare for them. That kind of preparation is important so that you can respond without stammering or stuttering. That helps to make the client more confident in you and more likely to award you the business. Face any objections head on, but do not belabor them. The client may simply be thinking out loud, and her objection may not be that significant.

You can determine if the prospect is just thinking out loud or has a significant objection. Restate her objection in the form of a question. For example, she may say, "I really hoped costs would not be this high." You could ask, "Are the costs I've presented more than you have budgeted or can afford?" or "What range did you expect costs for this project to be?"

If the prospect has a concern, restate it, and articulate how you can overcome the problem. Then ask something like, "Does that clarify things for you?" or "Do you understand?"

Sometimes people say they understand, but they don't. If she says she doesn't understand or if she looks like she doesn't, restate the problem or concern again and find a different way to explain how you can overcome it. As I said, don't belabor it, because if the client was only thinking out loud, you might just be talking her into really being concerned.

Concluding the Meeting

As the meeting concludes, sum up its key points. These likely will have been the key points of your presentation. Also, re-address any significant objections or concerns the prospect raised, giving your best suggestions to overcoming the objections or assuaging her concerns. You are almost done, but you still need to ask a couple more critical questions.

If you don't already know, ask who else is bidding on the project. This will help you understand how the prospect perceives you and the niche you fill.

Ask how your proposal stacks up against the other competitors. Be careful how you phrase this. You are looking for three things—the benefits of the other proposals that the prospect favors, the objections the prospect has of the other proposals, and the additional objections about your proposal that the prospect may not have addressed or may have been unwilling to bring up.

You should again ask if she has any other questions. This is probably your last shot at uncovering information, so pay attention. If you have done your job properly, however, the odds are she won't have anything else to ask. If she doesn't, underscore all the things about the presentation to which your prospect reacted favorably.

Then, Ask for the Business!

You must ask one more question. Take a deep breath, and *ask for the business*. You absolutely must, must, must do this. You have come this far, so you owe it to yourself and to the prospect. "But if I ask for it, they might be offended!" you protest.

She wouldn't have asked you to develop a proposal if you didn't have a shot at the project. Also, I can guarantee that if you don't ask for the business, the prospect almost *never* becomes a client.

It is very likely that the prospect will simply defer the decision, perhaps to review the proposals again with a colleague or higher up, or she might just be uncomfortable making the decision on the spot. So if she doesn't award you the business, simply conclude the meeting by thanking her for her time and reiterating that you appreciate the opportunity to present your capabilities and you hope to help her on the project. Then leave.

The Presentation Doesn't End in the Conference Room

When you get back to the office, you still have a couple more chores to do related to the presentation. The most important thing is to write a thank-you letter or card to the prospect. What you say in the card or letter is determined by how the meeting went.

If the meeting was very comfortable, a simple personal note might do just fine. I often send a handwritten card that has my company logo on it. In the card I thank the prospect for her time and reiterate how much I would like to work with her. Don't overcomplicate your correspondence. Just say thanks and add a personal comment if you think it's appropriate.

If the meeting carried a more formal business tone, then you are probably better off sending a letter. Unless there are very compelling reasons to include a lot of information, do not write a letter longer than a single page.

Again, thank the prospect for her time and reiterate how much you want to be selected to do the project. You should also reiterate the key points of the meeting and point out once again why you are the best candidate for the project. Then tell the prospect to expect your call at a specific time to answer any additional questions she or her colleagues may have about your proposal. Of course, keep the door open for her to call you, too. The letter and the phone call are just additional opportunities for you to make another positive impression on the prospect.

No News Is Bad News

Generally, I have found that if a prospect doesn't call you within seven to ten days of the presentation, what you—and perhaps your competitors—offered her wasn't compelling enough to move her to a buying decision.

A friend owns a small advertising agency that handled a large insurance company for over 25 years. A new advertising director for the insurance company came in. The new director called for a review of the agency's work and then put the account up for grabs. My friend's agency still appeared to be the front-runner because it was the incumbent and knew all about the client's business. The new advertising director said he wanted to have a look at what other agencies might do for his company.

Three agencies made presentations. Then everyone sat back to wait and wait and wait. The advertising director began sending out work to each of the agencies piecemeal—a brochure here, a radio spot there and so on. Ultimately, none of those agencies wound up as the agency of record with the insurance company. The advertising director awarded the business to one that wasn't part of the original three bidding agencies.

Why? Obviously my friend's agency and his competitors never gave the advertising director enough of a reason to make him want to hire one company over another. That left the door open for yet another company to come in and successfully romance him.

Which leads me to something I have alluded to throughout the book. Never give up. Even if you are swamped by meeting the needs of your current clients and are having trouble staying in touch, make a phone call once every couple of weeks to your hottest prospects. Always stay on top of those tasks related to developing new business.

How To Take Bad News

If the prospect doesn't call, don't take that personally either. Often enough the prospect may want to avoid either disappointing you or justifying why she selected another company or both. So you won't get called at all.

If the prospect calls you with bad news, keep your chin up because you still have some important work. You need to discover why the competitor got the job and you didn't. If there was more than one competitor, also try to find out why the other group or groups didn't get the job.

This can be very difficult information to glean. As I said, a prospect may simply not want to deliver the bad news or may not want to disappoint you. The decision may not have been based on logic at all. It may have been a gut-level decision. Some people won't tell you because they don't want to say why they selected someone else. Sometimes you don't have the experience they are looking for.

The Red Tie—Blue Tie Conundrum

In my business, because virtually all of my projects are prototypes, my clients and prospects are looking for someone who has very nearly done the work they need. I call this the red tie–blue tie conundrum.

I'll get a call from a prospect asking if we have ever done a videotape about ties. "We sure have," I'll say. "Really?" they respond. "Have you done one about red ties?" "No," I'll say, "but I have done one about blue ties." "Oh, thanks anyway. We really wanted someone who has done something about red ones." They hang up and continue looking for a company that has produced award-winning projects about red ties. Sometimes people won't hire you because you have not done exactly the kind of work they are looking for. Unfortunately, that's life.

When the Prospect Becomes the Client

What happens when the prospect calls with the good news that you have been awarded the job? That's when the fun begins. After all, that's what all of your hard work has been about.

Once you get the good news, you must set the client's expectations. The best time to do that is when you begin discussing the particulars of the project—things like deliverables and due dates—because you both still wear a honeymoon glow anticipating the pleasures of a project done well. But you must determine important elements of the project. If the client committed her graphic department's support to the project, remind her of that when you are talking about deliverables. Get details from her about who will be responsible internally to ensure that you get what you need. Then determine a course to take if the department cannot follow through on your client's promise.

Deliver More Than You Promise

Having set the client's expectations of what you will deliver, do your best to exceed them. Remember, every job you deliver when you are self-employed is an audition for the next project. Now, you are ready to move on to the next step: Making them want to hire you again.

CHAPTER 13

Making Them Want To Hire You Again

Success is never guaranteed, but there are two things that can help you increase the likelihood of succeeding. If you are doing something that you truly enjoy, you will probably do it with vigor and enthusiasm that others might not have. Also, if you can find a niche and do your business very well, people will seek you out.

When I worked for the bank, I gained a lot of experience on a variety of projects. Often, however, I was picked to produce a project outside of my expertise because I was on staff. Besides video projects, I wound up producing conferences, multi-image projects and radio spots. As I planned my own business, I expected to sell my video and film experience, but also those other skills I had acquired. On my own, I had some early success producing conferences and radio spots, but my strong suit was producing and directing corporate videos and films. I had the easiest time selling video and film production. Ultimately, that's all I sold.

Why? On my own there were very few opportunities just handed to me as there were when I was on staff. As I became more successful producing corporate films and videos, my reputation grew, and people called me just for that kind of work. The result? If someone calls me now about producing conferences and so on, I refer them to colleagues. I realize my skill set and have created a niche that keeps me very busy.

On top of that, people hire me to do what I do. They don't hire me to hire people who do what I do. I am in the service business, so I should be the one who is providing the service.

In fact, there are four adages that define my customer service philosophy. I believe in them whole heartedly, and I also believe that doing so keeps me working.

Adage #1: "You Can't Fall on Your Face If You Bend Over Backwards"

This very nearly speaks for itself. When my clients want something from me or if they want something changed, I do whatever I can to try to fulfill their requests.

Bending over backwards for your client doesn't mean being spineless, however. You have to be careful not to train your clients to expect they will get whatever they ask for—no matter how expensive the request.

One of my very first independent projects was a success in terms of meeting the project's communications objectives. It was a failure because I bent too far backwards for my client.

Actually, there were two clients: an engineer and her boss. I won the project because we provided the most bang for the buck. She told me so. Unfortunately, my inexperience shone through almost immediately—starting with my estimate. It was flawed. Right off the bat, I was making less money than I anticipated.

Still, the project proceeded fairly smoothly, though the client didn't come through on some things she promised for the project. I incurred additional expense because she failed to meet those obligations. Since I was happy to be working on the project, I let those things go. She and her boss reviewed and approved the script, and we began production.

After three days, we finished shooting. The next step was to create a rough version of the program so the client and her boss could approve the program's content. They had approved the script with a certain number of specific graphics, but after seeing the rough cut, they decided to add more. Though more graphics meant additional cost, I figured to absorb that, too. Worse, I didn't say anything.

They approved the rough cut, but they wanted some more changes adding some more costs to the project. In for a penny, in for a pound, I thought to myself, so I stayed mum about that.

My client attended the edit session, and she approved the additional changes they requested. When we finished, we showed a copy of the program to her boss. He wanted to make "just a few more changes." By this time, however, they had used up all of the budget—including the very modest contingency. I told him so. I also said that I would be glad to make the changes—for an additional charge. "But you made the changes we asked for and never said anything about running out of money," he protested.

He was right. I didn't have the experience to say anything to them. I was excited just to be doing the work. Along the way, as they asked for changes that were beyond the original scope of the job, I should have explained what the changes would mean to their time line and to the budget. I didn't. I just wanted to make certain they were pleased with the project. The irony is that in trying to please them by not talking about the monetary impact the changes brought, I sacrificed my relationship with them when I finally stopped giving them things that were outside of the project's original scope.

I felt that since they were the clients, I should bend over backwards and give them whatever they asked for. I was only half-right. When bending over backwards for a client, let her know what the gymnastics mean to you or to her budget and time line.

Now, if a client asks for changes, I do several things. I determine the impact the request has on the budget and the schedule, and whether the change is worthwhile. In other words, will fulfilling that request be beneficial to the project's communications objectives or will it be detrimental? Is the request small compared to the value of the client relationship or the money being spent on the project? Can I get it done within the time frame the client has set, or can I delegate it?

Having examined the request from those angles, I provide the client with options. I also explain the ramifications of each option and my recommendation or recommendations.

In the end, I do everything within my means to ensure that the client feels like she got exactly what she wanted. I very rarely tell my clients something isn't possible. As a result, they know that we can't do something if I say we can't.

Adage #2: "A Little Pie Beats No Pie"

You must know what you need to make to stay in business, too. You need to know for two reasons: To know what business you must walk away from, and to understand how sharp you need to make your pencil in order to get the business.

"A little pie beats no pie" is something I remember when someone asks us to do a project for less money than we would like to make but for more money than we would walk away from. If we have time open on the calendar—and we can usually find some time—we do the job. It gives us an opportunity to build a stronger client base.

One other justification to take a project that might bring you less than you normally make is that you hope the client will recognize your true worth and pay you more the next time there is a project. Unfortunately, not all clients think that way. So if you are doing a project for that very reason, let the client know—diplomatically—that you are working for less than what you normally charge, and that you expect the client to budget your expense appropriately on the next project.

What is your bottom line? You can bet your client knows what her bottom line is. No volume of business can make up for giving your work away.

Many a "consultant's consultant" says never to negotiate your rate. Hogwash. This is America. Everything is negotiable. But if your client or prospect is asking you to give up something, it's only fair to ask them to give up something.

For example, a high-tech company wanted me to direct two programs over ten days near their company headquarters. In addition to paying me less than I normally charge, they also warned me that their attorneys advised them to withhold payroll taxes from vendors like me—further reducing my take home. On top of that, their headquarters are about 90 miles from my office. If I took the job, I would be driving three hours per day on top of the ten or more hours per day that I would be working on the project. I was a little cool towards taking it, but I thought of a scenario that would make taking the assignment more desirable. Since my client was asking me to take less than I normally charged, I asked her if she would pay for my hotel and meal accommodations.

Corporations are funny. They often don't want to pay people, but they will pay people's expenses—even extraordinary ones. My expenses weren't extraordinary, and her company was willing to pick up my expenses. So, instead of driving 90 miles to work, I drove about three blocks from the hotel to the studio. As an added bonus, my wife and son stayed with me.

On the other hand, you also have to be careful about taking a job just to take it. Doing so might prevent you from getting other, better-paying projects or properly developing a proposal for that prospect you have been trying for months to turn into a client.

A little pie does beat no pie. Still, know your bottom line so you know when to pass up desert.

Pretend You're a Buyer

Say you want to buy a brand new car. You walk into the dealership, passing gleaming vehicles. Whirligigs spin. Banners flap. A sign on the window announces a great financing rate.

You feel good because you have done your homework. You know what you are willing to pay for a brand new model with the options you want because you've been to the library and you've shopped around for the last three months.

The dealer has established a price that he wants you to pay for the car, and he puts a sticker in the window to reinforce that price. After a test drive and some tire kicking, you and the salesman head into a cubicle to discuss the price. The salesman makes several trips back and forth to the sales manager. The two of you finally arrive on a price that pleases you both, so you sign on the dotted line. Then the salesman tells you how you "stole" the car at that price. Not likely.

The dealership knows what it needs to make on the car to pay for the staff salaries, the commission, the flooring contract, the whirligigs and the building. In other words, they know what they must make on each car they sell in order to stay open. If you refuse to pay at least that, they'll more than likely refuse to sell you the car.

Obviously, different dealerships work in different ways. High-volume dealerships that sell a lot of cars can afford to sell them for less money. Low-volume dealerships may need to make more money on each sale. In both cases, the successful dealerships stay in business because they know their bottom lines.

Adage #3: "The Phone Rings for My Pleasure—Work and a Paycheck"

No client request is too bothersome if you really consider the ultimate outcome. So when a client calls with a need, try to help.

When I was on staff, we had a secretary who used to whine whenever the telephone rang. She never seemed to realize that without the telephone ringing, we weren't doing business. Without business, we're out on the street.

It's even more important when you are self-employed. So, answer your phone before it rings a fourth time and answer with enthusiasm. If you are already on your other line talking with another client or prospect, don't be afraid to let your answering machine or system pick up the call. But return the call promptly.

I change my outgoing message daily (or more frequently if necessary) to let my clients, prospects and vendors know at the very least when they can expect my return call. If I am out, but can be reached, I leave that number. I also remind the caller that I can be paged.

Since the phone rings for my pleasure—work and a pay-check—I do whatever I can to get the phone to ring.

Adage #4: "We Are Working Because the Customer's Doors Are Open"

When you are working at a client's location, ease the impact you have on that environment. When I shoot a videotape at a client's store or facility or office, I always sit down with the person in charge of the location's operations to let them know what we plan to do and why we need to do it that way, and to discuss alternatives if that person has a problem with any of my plans.

In short, the best calling card you can leave behind is the positive experiences of the people in the company you did the work for.

Nobody "Owes" You the Work

When I was on staff, I mistakenly thought that "they" owed me for my effort. Of course, I was wrong. When I went out on my own and visited companies, I saw many people who thought the same way I had. I am embarrassed to admit that in my early days of self-employment I continued to carry that mistaken philosophy with me.

Because business took off nearly right off the bat, I figured that this was going to be just like working for a living without the pain-in-the-neck policies and meetings.

When I hit my first slump, I realized that I had to make people want to hire me again and again and again. It also made me realize that you have to treat everyone you work with as though he or she is your immediate client. From the person you greet at the front desk to the head of the company to the person who is buying your services, each person's opinion of you and your company is critical to getting hired again.

People in positions above and below your client move on, often into positions where they can hire you. At the very least, they can recommend people they know. This has happened to me on many occasions.

Get Evaluations of Your Work

Companies hire self-employed professionals because we are temporary. That means if the project doesn't go well or if we aren't quite what the client expected, we don't get hired again. No muss, no fuss from the personnel side.

I noticed this when I was on staff. Colleagues who were unhappy with someone's work might "lose" that person's business card. Often the infraction that caused this was some minor misunderstanding—something that would have been worked through if the independent was part of the staff.

When I went out on my own, I wanted to prevent such misunderstandings from happening to me so that I could get hired as frequently as possible. I created a ratings form, much like the one the bank used when my boss performed an evaluation of my work. After a project I send the form along with an addressed, stamped envelope to every key person involved in the project on the client's side. I ask them to rate my performance on a scale from one to six and encourage them to add their own comments.

For obvious reasons, it is important to me that my vendors are successful when they work on a project with me. To ensure that I do everything I can to help them succeed, I also ask them for feedback on how I met their needs during the project.

The first example on page 147 is my client evaluation.

I send evaluations separately from any other correspondence, and I always include a stamped self-addressed envelope.

The evaluation form on page 148 is one I ask my vendors to fill out.

Evaluations are important because they are useful in getting the client to tell me if I or my vendors did anything on the project that could have been improved or should have been changed, or to get the vendors to suggest ways I can reduce my expenses or to do things faster or better.

Remember that I advised you to ask the prospect about things she wished her current vendors might change? This is the other side of that coin. Ask your clients if there is anything in your relationship that they want you to change.

October 5, 1997

Donna Cavalin
Marketing and Promotions Manager
Industrial Facilities
25001 Industrial Boulevard
Novato, CA 94545

Dear Donna,

As an independent supplier of corporate communications, I don't have someone who regularly evaluates my work. It also means I must maintain a high level of service. To do that, I need your feedback. I would appreciate your honest evaluation of my efforts producing your recent project.

		(Circle one) High Low
QUALITY	Please rate my overall quality of service on this project.	6 5 4 3 2 1
IMPORTANCE	How important was my creative support in helping you attain your communications objectives?	6 5 4 3 2 1
TIMELINESS	How timely was I in meeting deadlines?	6 5 4 3 2 1
EFFECTIVENESS	Please rank the effectiveness of my creative support in reaching your objectives.	6 5 4 3 2 1
PROFESSIONAL INITIATIVE	Please rate my overall professional initiative in helping to meet this project's communications objectives.	6 5 4 3 2 1

Please use the reverse side to note additional comments. Thanks, in advance, for your feedback.

Greg

October 5, 1997

David Michaels
95 Intruder Lane—A6
Alameda, CA

Dear David:

Thanks for your help recently on Apple Computer's project. As you are well aware, I am an independent producer of creative communications, which means I want to maintain a high level of service. To do that, I need feedback from clients and key members of my team. I would appreciate it if you would take a moment to give me some feedback on our last job together. Doing so will give me insight on how to make your job and my job easier and our product better on the next project. Please feel free to use the back side of this form for additional comments or questions.

		(Circle one) **High Low**
COMMUNICATION	Please rate my communication with you on this project.	6 5 4 3 2 1
ORGANIZATION	Was the project well thought out, planned and organized?	6 5 4 3 2 1
EXECUTION	Was the project well executed?	6 5 4 3 2 1
EFFECTIVENESS	Please rate the effectiveness of my creative support and production in meeting your production needs.	6 5 4 3 2 1
QUALITY	Please rate the overall professional quality of this project.	6 5 4 3 2 1

Enclosed is a stamped, self-addressed envelope for your convenience. Thanks, in advance, for your feedback.

Greg

As you undertake your project with those client service philosophies imbedded in your efforts, you must also realize that you will be working with a variety of people—people you bring in, people who work with and for your client, and the client—throughout the process.

CHAPTER 14

Winning Strategies for All the People You Work With

Along the way, projects will require that you bring other vendors in to work on the project with you. Projects may also require that you work with people on the client's staff. Of course, you are going to be working closely at points along the way with the client, too. Since every job is an audition for the next one, how you work with everyone has a significant effect on whether you get asked back.

Bringing Your People to the Project

The people you bring to the project are critical to your own success. Whether they are vendors, subcontractors or temporary staff, make certain that you hire only those people who are capable and willing to give their very best for you. The relationship between you and your vendors must always be positive. Also, the relationship between your vendors and the client and client's staff must also be good. If there is rancor between you and your people, or between two or more of them, it will reflect badly on you. Of course, if your vendors appear inept, your client relationship can be jeopardized.

Your own relationship with your vendors begins when you negotiate with them about their fees. Remember that when you talk about money and deliverables with them.

Negotiating Fees with Your People

There are three possible ways to negotiate rates. One way is to ask a person what his rate is. He tells you, and then you proceed to whittle him down to the raw bone. Another way is to honestly and forthrightly tell the person how much you have budgeted for the work. Then you can begin the give and take from there. The third way is to ask the vendor what he charges and pay that rate.

Having worked for people who negotiate by squeezing every drop of blood from me, I am seldom completely happy about having agreed to the fee. Negotiating this way is saying to the vendor, "You are not worth to me as much as you think you are worth."

As a rule, I want people working for me who have pride in their work and who bring a real value to the project by their participation. I try to give them what they believe they are worth.

Sometimes, what I have budgeted for a vendor's role is less than what that vendor wants. If so, I offer the amount I have budgeted and let the vendor know that if he doesn't want to work for that rate, I won't take it personally. Usually, my relationship with the vendor carries weight, and the vendor will work with me. Of course, if I am asking my vendors to work for less, then I work for less as well.

If a vendor signs on for the project, I expect that he will give me 100 percent. My vendors should work as hard for me as I do for the client. If a vendor doesn't, I will speak with him about it. If things don't improve, I don't waste any time in finding someone else to replace him.

Treating the Client's Staff Like They're the Client

One of the differences between working on staff and being self-employed is that as an independent you often get to hand-pick the people with whom you want to work. Sometimes, however, a client may want you to work with people she chooses. Whatever reason she has for assigning someone to you for the project, treat that person the same way you would treat the client.

People on the client's staff are as important to your success as your vendors. Though they might be helping you or literally working for you on the project, each of these people is also your client. It's important to discover what makes them tick, too. Unlike your vendors, however, they are not concerned that you hire them again. So they don't have the same loyalty to you as your vendors.

From the client's secretary or administrative assistant to the company's most senior staff, it is imperative that they perceive you as competent, capable, pleasant and worth far more than the fee you are charging. Again, the best calling card you can leave behind is the good feelings about the work you did.

Overcoming Potential Problems with the Client's Staff

As I said earlier, sometimes people who are on staff have an "owe me" attitude. This negative attitude can be caused by a variety of things. The person's boss may be seen as a bad guy, so the staffer fights back with the only power he has—indifference or worse.

There's another employee attitude that can torpedo your ship. A fellow I used to work with called it "malicious obedience."

Malicious obedience is when cohorts do as they are told regardless of the outcome they know their actions will bring. You'll usually find acts of malicious obedience occurring in offices where a boss restricts the staff's ability to make proactive decisions or to take independent action themselves. The staff is left only with the authority to say "No" to tasks that are outside of their job responsibilities. Your requests for help can be answered with an "it's not my table" attitude.

Other problems stem from internal policies. For example, I try to work as quickly and efficiently as I can. After all, time is money. If I can finish a project sooner than expected, I'm ahead. There have been times when doing a video for a company's in-house production group that I find myself with just an hour or so of editing left to complete the project. But many corporation's don't want to pay overtime or compensatory time, so the bosses insist that people go home at a specific hour. That means I have to return the next day to wrap things up, and that means it will take longer than the hour, because of the morning routines—people chatting about last night's television show, getting coffee or exchanging the latest office gossip. Often, there's very little I can do about it except live with it.

Other times, someone on the client's staff has her own agenda. She may fly a stealth bomber targeting smart bombs on your project. The client may only see the destruction and perceive it as something you induced. The best way to keep that from happening to you is to treat everyone on staff as you would the client.

One of the worst things that can happen to you is getting someone assigned from the staff to work in a key position on the project who is not competent in that particular role. This can happen if the client is trying to manage the person out— building up a case to fire the staffer—or if the client needs to get the incompetent person out of another key role on some other project.

Of course, these are worst-case scenarios that are important to be on the lookout for. Most of the time, people on staff care just as much about their work as you do. Regardless of how you work with people on the client's staff, if you treat each of them the way you would treat your client, you'll increase your odds for success.

Building a Golden Relationship with Your Client

The most important relationship in your life next to the one with your spouse or significant other is with your client. The relationship is golden and must be treated so. In many ways, the rules for a successful marriage apply in your client relationships.

The most important element in a client relationship is the trust the client has in your ability to do the work. That means you need to ensure the project meets its objectives, is brought in on time and is completed within budget.

Two Golden Rules

1. Always deliver more than you promise.
2. Always deliver earlier than you promise.

Support your client's business objectives. Be aware that the client may have personal objectives, too, so support them.

Be open and honest in your dealings with the client. An advertising agency that I managed some projects for was handling the communications programs for a retirement community. The agency ultimately resigned the account because they couldn't justify the charges they were billing the retirement community. Also, don't give the client an estimate knowing that you will add costs because of the client's inexact or inappropriate job specs.

Be courteous and thoughtful. Remember birthdays and anniversaries. Congratulations are always in order; give them freely.

Be ethical—with everyone.

Be on time. Never be the one for whom people are waiting. If you know someone is always running behind, plan to make some calls, write thank-you notes or make use of the time you have while you're waiting.

Thank the client when she does something nice for you. Try to return the favor.

The Easiest Prospect To Land Is Your Current Client

Whenever you are in your client's office, keep your eyes and ears open for ways to help her. You'll be creating opportunities for yourself at the same time. During the course of conversation, she might mention or describe upcoming projects or needs. Ask for the opportunity to work on those projects or how you can fill those needs. If you have a good relationship, she might very well give you the project right there because she can get that task off her already overloaded to-do list. Remember, you can be both an order-taker and an order-maker. For example, when I was on staff, we had one vendor who very often was working on the proposal for one project while he was finishing another.

After you finish your project, don't forget to thank your client for the work. There are plenty of vendors out there, and she didn't have to hire you. Let her know how much you appreciated working with her. Treat her to lunch. While you're both enjoying your meal, ask for new business. You'll be surprised how often you'll get more opportunities.

Try to never burn your bridges. There are times when working with anyone that the "marriage" just goes bad. If that happens to you—and sooner or later it will—try to extricate yourself from the scene without completely cutting off your relationship with the client. You may need a reference from the client later. Maybe time will heal the "wound," and you'll want to work with the client or the client will need you for a project down the road.

I wish I could say that I always listen to my own advice, but there was one unfortunate situation in my career when I pushed the plunger and destroyed the bridge. It happened because of a misunderstanding over money. The relationship was already deteriorating, so communication between us was difficult. I regret that it happened because once you destroy the bridge, it's very difficult to cross back over the river. Worse, news travels fast—bad news travels at the speed of light. Destroying a bridge makes you look bad within your own community of clients, colleagues and suppliers.

Delivering Bad News

A project always sets sail with a marching band at the pier, lots of speeches by officials, and the wish for fair winds and following seas. But the weather doesn't always hold up. Gale winds blow, the seas swell and your boat takes on water. On top of that, you lose your mainsail. The whole project enters the Bermuda Triangle, and the crew and vessel are lost forever. When that happens, you have to tell the backers of the expedition.

How do you deliver bad news?

First, familiarize yourself with all aspects of it. Second, develop a list of worst-case/best-case scenarios. What are the costs involved? What impact will the problem have on the project's schedule? What resources do you have to help deal with the problem? What resources does the client have to help deal with it?

If you can resolve the problem yourself, you should immediately take care of it. Then if the client needs to know that there even was a problem, let her know.

If you can't resolve the problem, determine what steps will be necessary to get the problem resolved? Once you have clarified all of the issues, talk to the client. If you can, deliver the news in person. If a delay may worsen the situation, use whatever means you can to tell the client about it. But you be the one to deliver the bad news.

Tell the client the extent of the problem. Tell the client why the problem happened. *Never* blame someone else. You are the captain of the ship, even if someone else ran it aground. Give the client optional ways the problem can be resolved, along with your recommendation of the best route to take.

Every time I think I have seen the biggest problem I'll ever face, something bigger comes along. Among the worst things that ever happened to me was on my inaugural project for a retailer.

When Disaster Strikes

- Determine the extent of the problem.
- Familiarize yourself with all aspects of it.
- Develop "worst-case" and "best-case" scenarios.
- Resolve it immediately if you can.
- If you can't, determine what needs to occur to resolve the problem
- Tell the client—in person if possible.
- Take responsibility, even if the problem was not your fault.
- Do everything in your power to see that the problem is resolved—even if it costs you time and money.

I had been pursuing the company for about two years, and I finally got my chance. It was a big project. I had several actors and a very large crew. We were shooting for three consecutive nights.

After we finished shooting, I took the master tapes to be copied. The copies allow me to make a preliminary version of the program for the client to approve. The original masters are saved for the final editing.

In the meantime, I was shooting a commercial for another client. During a break in that production, I checked with my office for messages. One was from the fellow who was making the copies. He said there "seemed to be a problem" with one of the tapes, and he wanted me to call him when I could. He didn't sound anxious, but I did get back to him quickly.

He explained that one of the tapes "looked funny," and he wanted me to stop by on my way home to check it out. I couldn't because of the commercial I was working on, but we arranged to meet the following morning.

When we did meet, I discovered that the one tape "looked funny" because his videotape machine *ate* my master tape. As I watched the monitor, then inspected the tape, my stomach left me. I felt sick. It seemed likely that I was not only going to lose a hard-won client, but I would also lose thousands of dollars. I was going to have to get the entire cast and crew back together for a reshoot.

Once I got my wits about me, I took the tape to some experts—some of the people in my network—to have them look at the tape to see if we could salvage it. No luck.

I took the tape to an editing facility to see if there was any way we could use special effects to make the tape useable. No luck.

I reviewed my script, notes from the shoot and tape logs to see if there was some way we could edit the program to avoid having to reshoot. Again, no luck.

I was out of questions, let alone answers. It was time to tell the client.

I said to him, "I have some bad news and some better news."

"What's that?" he asked.

"One of the master tapes has been destroyed because of a faulty tape machine," I said. "We'll have to reshoot. It won't cost you anything except the inconvenience of staying up all night again."

Then I went on to describe in detail what was actually wrong with the tape. I also described who I talked with to resolve the problem and what little could actually be done about the problem. My client agreed that the only way to make it right was to reshoot, so we scheduled another night's work.

The story ended much better than I expected it to end. The company that destroyed the tape had insurance which covered my loss. Better yet, my client became a good one because he realized I could and would back up my work. He told me later that he never had any qualms about working with me again because he knew I could deliver what I promised.

You know that you are successfully self-employed when things go awry and your client still calls you back for more projects. In the end, our goal is to get asked back by every client. Doing that means we build our client base.

CHAPTER 15

Making Success a Habit

I hope that what I have described in the previous chapters has convinced you that selling professional services is not as complicated as many people make it out to be. It's really a step-by-step process that, if followed, virtually guarantees you will build a strong client base, adapt to changing market conditions, be successfully self-employed and thrive.

The information I've provided in this book is based on my own personality and industry. You'll need to adapt what you've learned here to your own style. If you aren't clear about what your style is, put yourself in some sales situations as the buyer and see what you like and what you don't like about each situation. That will help you discover your style. Then begin to make this information yours, and you are well on your way to becoming successfully self-employed.

As I said in the Acknowledgments at the beginning of the book, success is measured in microns. Consider each minuscule step forward as a marker of success. Remember that you need to make enough positive impressions on enough people so some of them will hire you—hopefully more than once.

Don't let fear of failure, fear of rejection or even fear of success get in your way. You can overcome those fears by realizing that when people don't let you tell them how you can help them, they are the ones who lose. No one can ever have enough good people helping or waiting to help them. If you have listened to the prospect or client well, and he still doesn't buy from you, you aren't being rejected personally. He just doesn't need the services you are offering. If he needs them but doesn't buy, he may not be able to afford them, or someone or something within his business may not let him buy your services.

Consider the entire process of selling professional services an inverted pyramid or a funnel that points you toward business.

Start by writing a business plan. Besides helping with the simple things like how to set up your office and with complex things like how to deal with changing markets, the business plan does some other important things. It makes you write down your goals and objectives so that you describe where you are going to look for business and how you are going to get it. Setting your goals and objectives helps you target specific industries to sell to, then target specific businesses in those industries and, finally, find and target the specific buyers in those businesses.

Plan your business. Plan your calls to your clients. Plan your calls on prospects. Plan your questions when you meet with clients and prospects. Plan your projects.

Remember that a plan lets you choose adapting or migrating over perishing. A plan is also something you can refer to when business isn't going exactly the way you think it should. Even with such a plan under your arm, don't be afraid to allow serendipity to have an effect on your business, too. By keeping your eyes open and your head on a swivel, by being pleasantly and curiously nosy about people, you're bound to run into business. Uncovering what kind of help someone needs lets you understand what kind of business you can do with her (or what kind of business someone else in your network can do).

Remember, too, that selling professional services doesn't necessarily mean that you need to have a huge volume of clients. I have been successful with just a few at any given time. On the other hand, always be looking to add a new client because people quit, get transferred, take maternity leave or otherwise go away.

Satisfied clients are the best way to develop your business. They are willing to hire you repeatedly. If they don't do a lot of work, they will often refer you to other business.

Also, 80 percent of your business will come from 20 percent of your clients. As you build your business, keep looking for clients who will be part of that 20 percent. Finding them will make your business grow.

When you are self-employed, your network is your lifeblood. Constantly tune your network, because from it will come business referrals and vendor support. Don't be a hermit. Get out and meet people for whom you can work. If you need a favor from a vendor, don't be afraid to ask. But don't be afraid to do a favor first. It will all balance out.

A prospect is very unlikely to talk with someone she doesn't know. Adapt and use the four-paragraph, single-page letter to get the prospect to take your call.

In the first paragraph, tell her who referred you or how you otherwise got her name. If a friend or colleague referred you, tell her that in the first paragraph.

In the second paragraph, describe how you believe you can help her. If you can use an example that is similar to projects she manages, so much the better.

In the third paragraph, tell the prospect other experiences you have had with other businesses in her company's industry. If you don't have that kind of experience, tell her about projects you have done that are similar to the kinds of work you think or know she needs.

In the fourth paragraph, make a contract with yourself to call the prospect at a specific time by telling her when to expect your call. Then make the call.

The letter is designed to get the prospect to take your call. Your call is designed to get the prospect to meet with you. When you call, don't forget important things like asking the prospect if it is a good time to talk. Reiterate the message in your introductory letter and have some questions planned to help prompt a discussion. You are developing a relationship with this prospect.

You have to meet with the prospect because you need to find out what she looks for in vendors and because you need to illustrate to her the work you do. Developing business is all about asking questions—the right questions. Ultimately, you need to ask, "Can we do business together?"

Perseverance is always helpful, but it's particularly important when you are just starting out on your own. It can take five calls or more on a prospect to turn her into a client.

Keeping your eyes and ears open is also important whenever you are in a prospect's or a client's office. In the prospect's office you'll likely find periodicals about her industry, her company, or other pertinent information that can give you some insight to help you get business. In the client's office, keeping your eyes and ears open may help you "make an order."

Especially in your first meeting with the prospect, listen 80 percent of the time and talk 20 percent. You can only find out what the prospect or client needs when she is telling you.

When you meet with a prospect for the first time, find out about the vendors she uses and why. Remember you have to find out what the prospect needs, find out what the prospect wants and find out what the prospect is willing to pay. Then, having determined those three things, assess and match her expectations of the end product with what you plan to deliver.

In your meeting don't forget to ask two critical questions: "If there was one thing you could change about the way your vendors are currently doing business, what would that be?" and "Do you have a project now or in the foreseeable future in which I could play a role?"

To convert the prospect into a client you have to ask for the business. If you don't ask for it, you won't get it. If you take nothing else away from reading this book, at least remember to *ask for the business*.

Of course, your best prospect for business comes from the client you already have. You know him, he knows you. Treat him as the goose who lays a golden egg, because that's exactly what he does for you.

While you are at it, treat everyone along the way as you would treat your client. From the administrative assistant to the CEO, your best calling card is their experience with you. If people have a good experience with you, they'll be interested in having another and another and another.

When it comes time to deliver your work, deliver more than you promised and earlier than you promised. If there are problems, own up to them and then find out what you can do to resolve them. Show the client that you can be counted on regardless of what happens.

You can only control so many things. Try not to worry about things you can't control. It's been said that 90 percent of what you worry about never happens anyway. The other 10 percent happens in a different way than you expect. Also, there's never anything wrong with being lucky, having things go your way. When they do, enjoy the ride.

Take each small victory and savor it. When I began writing this book, I thought it would be somewhat like winning the Publishers Clearing House Grand Prize. People would show up at my door during halftime of the Super Bowl with cameras rolling and present me with a check. Instead, it was a series—and I do mean a series—of barely incremental victories.

First, there was the gestation period when I thought about writing this. When I started actually writing the book, I had a couple of false starts. Finally I wrote an outline to build a framework for the content, and this thing really got underway. After I completed the first draft, I contacted over 50 agents to represent me. Several responded positively. The agent who took me on board had me write five drafts of the book proposal. Then she submitted the proposal to over a dozen publishers, and I went back to working on the book again. Now that the book is published, I am out telling people about it, encouraging them to buy a copy. As I said, success is really a process of incremental steps forward—and an occasional stumble backwards.

That ties in to what I have laced throughout the book. Never give up. Persevere. Just try to get to the plate more often. The more you get to bat, the more likely you will get a hit. The more hits you get, then the more likely you are to score, and the more likely that you will thrive as someone who is successfully self-employed.

INDEX